# First World War
### and Army of Occupation
# War Diary
### France, Belgium and Germany

9 DIVISION
3 Lowland Brigades
Headquarters
1 April 1919 - 9 September 1919

WO95/1776/10

The Naval & Military Press Ltd
www.nmarchive.com
**Published in association with The National Archives**

Published by

## The Naval & Military Press Ltd

Unit 10 Ridgewood Industrial Park,

Uckfield, East Sussex,

TN22 5QE England

Tel: +44 (0) 1825 749494

www.naval-military-press.com

www.nmarchive.com

*This diary has been reprinted in facsimile from the original. Any imperfections are inevitably reproduced and the quality may fall short of modern type and cartographic standards.*

**© Crown Copyright**
**Images reproduced by permission of The National Archives, London, England, 2015.**

# Contents

| Document type | Place/Title | Date From | Date To |
|---|---|---|---|
| Heading | Lowland (Late 9) Division HQ 3rd Lowland Bde 1919 Apr-1919 Sep | | |
| War Diary | Benrath | 01/04/1919 | 30/04/1919 |
| War Diary | Benrath Germany | 01/05/1919 | 31/05/1919 |
| War Diary | Benrath | 01/06/1919 | 30/06/1919 |
| Miscellaneous | Amendment No.1 To 3rd Lowland Brigade Order No.1 | 10/06/1919 | 10/06/1919 |
| Operation(al) Order(s) | 3rd Lowland Brigade Order No.1 | 26/05/1919 | 26/05/1919 |
| Miscellaneous | Table A.1 Attached To Amendment No.1 To 3rd Lowland Bde Order No.1 | | |
| Miscellaneous | Appendix "B" to be Attached to 3rd Lowland Brigade Order No.1 | 17/06/1919 | 17/06/1919 |
| Map | Superimpose C | | |
| Operation(al) Order(s) | 3rd Lowland Brigade Order No.2 | 18/06/1919 | 18/06/1919 |
| Miscellaneous | Table "A" Attached To 3rd Lowland Brigade Order No.2 | | |
| Miscellaneous | 3rd Lowland Brigade Instructions No.2 | 17/06/1919 | 17/06/1919 |
| Miscellaneous | Administrative Instructions No.1 | 17/06/1919 | 17/06/1919 |
| Miscellaneous | 3rd Lowland Infantry Brigade Administrative Instructions No.1 | 17/06/1919 | 17/06/1919 |
| Miscellaneous | 3rd Lowland Brigade Instructions No.1 | 17/06/1919 | 17/06/1919 |
| Operation(al) Order(s) | 3rd Lowland Brigade Order No.6 | 25/06/1919 | 25/06/1919 |
| Miscellaneous | 3rd Lowland Brigade Instructions No.3 | 19/06/1919 | 19/06/1919 |
| Miscellaneous | 3rd Lowland Brigade Instructions No.4 | 20/06/1919 | 20/06/1919 |
| Miscellaneous | 1st Line Transport And Baggage Wagons March Time Table Attached To 3rd Lowland Bde. Order No.1 | | |
| Miscellaneous | March Time Table Infantry & Artillery | | |
| Operation(al) Order(s) | 3rd Lowland Brigade Order No.3 | 23/06/1919 | 23/06/1919 |
| War Diary | Benrath | 01/07/1919 | 07/07/1919 |
| War Diary | Bedburg | 08/07/1919 | 31/07/1919 |
| Miscellaneous | 3rd Lowland Infantry Brigade | 06/04/1919 | 06/04/1919 |
| Miscellaneous | 3rd Lowland Infantry Brigade Administrative Instructions No.1 | 06/07/1919 | 06/07/1919 |
| Miscellaneous | 3rd Lowland Brigade Table A | | |
| Operation(al) Order(s) | 3rd Lowland Brigade Order No.1 | 06/07/1919 | 06/07/1919 |
| War Diary | Bedburg | 01/08/1919 | 31/08/1919 |
| Miscellaneous | General Instructions No.1 | 29/08/1919 | 29/08/1919 |
| Miscellaneous | 3rd Lowland Infantry Brigade Table "A" Issued With General Instructions No.1 | | |
| Miscellaneous | 3rd Lowland Infantry Brigade Table "B" Issued With General Instructions No.1 | | |
| War Diary | Bedburg Germany | 01/09/1919 | 09/09/1919 |

# LOWLAND (LATE 9) DIVISION

## HQ 3rd LOWLAND BDE

### 1919 APR - 1919 SEP

Army Form C. 2118.

HQ 3 Jordan Inf Bde

No 8

# WAR DIARY
## or
## INTELLIGENCE SUMMARY.
*(Erase heading not required.)*

Instructions regarding War Diaries and Intelligence Summaries are contained in F. S. Regs., Part II. and the Staff Manual respectively. Title pages will be prepared in manuscript.

| Place | Date | Hour | Summary of Events and Information | Remarks and references to Appendices |
|---|---|---|---|---|
| BENRATH | 1/4/19. | | Wiring of Defence Line continued. Annual Training Commenced. | M.M. |
| | 2/4/19. | | 'Retainable personnel, of 1st London Scottish left HILDEN and proceeded to 30th Division. Divisional Commander, accompanied by B.G.C. inspected Examining Posts. 'B' Coy 9th S.R. O Replay of Divisional 'Best' Company Competition resulted in a draw. 90th Field Coy O. | M.M. |
| | 3/4/19. | | 'Cadre of 2nd R.S.F. left Brigade for U.K. Brigade Commander inspected Railway Control Post at REISHOLZ station. Training was carried out as usual. | M.M. |
| | 4/4/19. | | 1/8th Sco. Rifles mounted Examining Guard in HIMMELGEIST. Brigade Commander rode round Examining Boards with Brigade Major. Wiring of Defence Line and Annual Training continued. | M.M. |
| | 5/4/19. | | Annual Training and Wiring of Defence Line continued. Orders issued instructing 1/8th Sco. Rifles to take over post at KEMPERDICK and DIEKHAUS from the 1/4th Ryl. Sco. Fusrs. on Wednesday 9th April. | M.M. |
| | 6/4/19. | | Church Services. | |

Army Form C. 2118.

# WAR DIARY
## or
## INTELLIGENCE SUMMARY.
(Erase heading not required.)

Instructions regarding War Diaries and Intelligence Summaries are contained in F. S. Regs., Part II. and the Staff Manual respectively. Title pages will be prepared in manuscript.

| Place | Date | Hour | Summary of Events and Information | Remarks and references to Appendices |
|---|---|---|---|---|
| BENRATH | 7/4/19. | | Cadre of 1st London Scottish proceeded to 8th Division on way to U.K. | nil |
| | | | Test of New Light Lewis-Guns carried out on Brigade Range. | nil |
| | | | Training and Wiring carried out. | nil |
| | 8/4/19. | | do           do | nil |
| | 9/4/19. | | do           do | nil |
| | 10/4/19. | | do           do | nil |
| | 11/4/19. | | B.G.C. attended conference at Divisional H.Q. Subject:-Defence Scheme. | nil |
| | | | Training and Wiring carried out. | |
| | | | Brigade Major and all Adjutants attended conference with G.S.O. at Divisional College. Subject:- Completing Battalions up to scale of O.B.1919. | nil |
| | | | Information received that conflict had taken place in DUSSELDORF between Government Troops and Spartacists. Acting under orders received from Division, precautionary measures were put into force. | |
| | 12/4/19. | | As situation in DUSSELDORF had quietened, the precautionary measures were removed. | nil |
| | | | Copies of Provisional Defence Scheme for 3rd (Lowland) Brigade issued to Battalions Field Coy and Field Ambulance. Brigade Commander held conference of Commanding Officers in connection with Defence Scheme. | |

Army Form C. 2118.

# WAR DIARY
## or
## INTELLIGENCE SUMMARY.
*(Erase heading not required.)*

Instructions regarding War Diaries and Intelligence Summaries are contained in F. S. Regs., Part II. and the Staff Manual respectively. Title pages will be prepared in manuscript.

| Place | Date | Hour | Summary of Events and Information | Remarks and references to Appendices |
|---|---|---|---|---|
| BENRATH | 13/4/19 | | Position in DUSSELDORF reported to be quieter. Sounds of heavy mortar fire distinctly heard at half - hourly intervals throughout the day. Lieut-Col.J.M.FINDLAY.D.S.O., arrived to take over command of 1/8th. Sco. Rifles. | nil |
| | 14/4/19 | | Brigadier General. E.S.GIRDWOOD proceeded to U.K.on one month's leave. Lieut-Col.W.V.LUMSDEN.D.S.O.9th.Sco.Rifles.assumed command of the 3rd.Lowland Brigade. | nil |
| | 15/4/19 | | Lieut-Colonel.J.L.JACK.D.S.O.9th.Sco.Rifles,returned from leave, and assumed command of 3rd.Lowland Brigade vice Lt.Col.W.V.LUMSDEN.D.S.O. Information received that Govt.Troops in DUSSELDORF had situation well in hand. | nil |
| | 16/4/19 | | Training etc carried out as usual. | nil |
| | 17/4/19 | | Conference in connection with Food Situation held at Brigade Headquarters Present:- Divisional Commanders,Brigade Commanders, Bde Intelligence (E) Officer and BURGOMASTER BENRATH. | nil |
| | 18/4/19. | | Holiday. Divisional Commander inspected Perimeter Examining Guards. | nil |
| | 19/4/19. | | Brigade Commander sited wire for the New Portion of Line of Resistance taken over from 2nd.Lowland Brigade. | nil |

Army Form C. 2118.

# WAR DIARY
## or
## INTELLIGENCE SUMMARY.
*(Erase heading not required.)*

Instructions regarding War Diaries and Intelligence Summaries are contained in F. S. Regs., Part II. and the Staff Manual respectively. Title pages will be prepared in manuscript.

| Place | Date | Hour | Summary of Events and Information | Remarks and references to Appendices |
|---|---|---|---|---|
| BENRATH | 20/4/19. | | Church Services:- | ACA |
| | 21/4/19. | | 1/4th.R.S.F. ordered to take over REISHOLZ Examining Guard from 9th.S.R. Holiday. | ACA |
| | 22/4/19. | | Brigade Commander held conference at Brigade Headquarters in connection with Defence Scheme and Training. Training carried out as usual. | ACA |
| | 23/4/19. | | Brigade Commander inspected Battalion Training. Training carried out as usual. | ACA |
| | 24/4/19. | | G.S.O.I. Lowland Division held conference at Divisional College. Brigade Majors. Staff Captains and Adjutants attended. | ACA |
| | 25/4/19. 26/4/19. | | Training etc carried out as usual. Captain.M.C.Morgan, South Wales Borderers took over the duties of Brigade Major from Captain.J.Hathorn.Hall. Royal Munster Fusiliers, who proceeded to England for demobilization. Church Services. | ACA ACA |
| | 27/4/19. | | Lieut-Colonel.Lockhead.Jack.D.S.O. temporary Brigade Commander, injured whilst racing in the London Division Races. | ACA |
| | 28/4/19. | | Training carried out as usual. Lieut-Colonel.Lockhead.Jack.D.S.O. admitted to 36 C.C.S. with dislocated shoulder blade. | ACA |
| | 29/4/19. | | Lieut-Colonel.W.V.Lumsden. D.S.O. M.C. 9th.Sco.Rifles assumed temporary command of the Brigade. | ACA |
| | 30/4/19. | | Wiring and usual training etc carried out. | ACA |

Lieut-Colonel,
Commanding 3rd. Lowland Brigade.

Army Form C. 2118.

# WAR DIARY
## or
## INTELLIGENCE SUMMARY.
*(Erase heading not required.)*

Instructions regarding War Diaries and Intelligence Summaries are contained in F. S. Regs., Part II. and the Staff Manual respectively. Title pages will be prepared in manuscript.

| Place | Date | Hour | Summary of Events and Information | Remarks and references to Appendices |
|---|---|---|---|---|
| BENRATH. | 1/5/19. | | Training carried out as usual. | |
| Germany. | 2/5/19. | | Training carried out as usual. | |
| | 3/5/19. | | Lt-Col.J.H.FINLAY.D.S.O.1/8th.Scottish Rifles assumed command of the Brigade. | |
| | 4-5-19. | | Church Parades. | |
| | 5/5/19. | | Training. Course for young Officers and N.C.O's commenced at HILDEN by Lieut MORRIS, 11.Corps School. | |
| | 6/5/19. | | Training as usual. | |
| | 7/5/19. | | Training as usual. | |
| | 8/5/19. | | Training as usual. | |
| | 9/5/19. | | Training as usual. Lecture delivered at HILDEN by Mr.J.McCABE on "Life in the Past Ages". | |
| | 10/5/19. | | Owing to rumoured strikes likely to take place 1/8th.Scottish Rifles ordered to supply a guard of 1.Platoon at the Electrical Power Station. | |
| | 11/5/19. | | Church Parade. | |
| | 12/5/19. | | Training as usual. | |
| | 13/5/19. | | Training as usual. 1.Company 5/6th.Royal Scots, ordered to be in readiness to move to 3rd.Lowland Brigade at short notice. | |

Army Form C. 2118.

# WAR DIARY
## *or*
## INTELLIGENCE SUMMARY.
(*Erase heading not required.*)

| Place | Date | Hour | Summary of Events and Information | Remarks and references to Appendices |
|---|---|---|---|---|
| BENRATH Germany. | 14/5/19. | | Strike threatened to take place on the 15th inst. In consequence 1.Company 5/6 Royal.Scots ordered to join the Brigade at BENRATH. H.Q. and 2 Companies 1/8th Scottish Rifles ordered to move from HILDEN to BENRATH by 6.p.m. | |
| | 15/5/19. | | Factories resumed work as usual. As a demonstration, all available troops including A/51st.Bde.R.F.A. made a marched demonstration through HILDEN and BENRATH. | |
| | 16/5/19. | | 1/8th.Scottish Rifles moved back to HILDEN. Lecture by Brigadier General.F.G. STONE. C.M.G. | |
| | 17/5/19. | | Company 5/6th.Royal Scots moved back to 2nd.Lowland Brigade to rejoin their Battalion. Brigadier General.E.S.GIRDWOOD. C.B. arrived back from leave and assumed command of the Brigade. | |
| | 18/5/19. | | Church Parades. Conference of Brigadiers' ordered at Divisional Headquarters. 10.a.m. | |
| | 19/5/19. | | Conference of C.O.'s' ordered at Brigade Headquarters 9-15 a.m. 9th.Scottish Rifles relieved on the outpost line by the 1/8th.Scottish Rifles at HOLTHAUSEN BARRIER. Disposition of the Brigade on the outpost line as follows:-<br>No.1.Post. KEMPERDICK. held by 1/4th.Ryl.Scots.Fusrs.<br>No.2.Post. DICKHAUS. held by the 1/4th.Ryl.Scots.Fusrs.<br>No.3.Post. REISHOLZ. held by 1/4th.Ryl.Scots.Fusrs.<br>No.4.Post. FREIDHOF. held by 1/4th.Ryl.Scots.Fusrs. | |

Army Form C. 2118.

# WAR DIARY
## or
## INTELLIGENCE SUMMARY.
*(Erase heading not required.)*

| Place | Date | Hour | Summary of Events and Information | Remarks and references to Appendices |
|---|---|---|---|---|
| BENRATH GERMANY. | 19/5/19 | | No.5.Post. HOLTHAUSEN. held by 1/8th.Scottish Rifles. No.6.Post. HIMMELGEIST-held by 1/8th.Scottish Rifles. | |
| | 20/5/19 | | Owing to more troops being required for the outpost line, Training in the Brigade has become very difficult. | |
| | 21/5/19 | | C-in-C visited an observation post near HILDEN. | |
| | 22/5/19. | | C-in-C ordered to meet C-in-C at 10-a.m. Conference held at Divisional H.Q. on the question of the advance in certain eventualities.B.G.C. B.M. S.C. ordered to attend. Brigade Major ordered to meet C-in-C at 10-a.m. | |
| | 23/5/19 | | Training as usual. Lecture delivered by Mr.KIRWAN in HILDEN on "In Shakespearian Atmospheres". Order No.3. received from Division. | |
| | 24/5/19 | | Training as usual. | |
| | 25/5/19 | | Church Parades. | |
| | 26/5/19 | | Training as usual. | |
| | 27/5/19 | | The Divisional Commander made an inspection of Billets, Cook-houses, Men's Messes, Battalion Institutes etc of all Battalions in the Brigade. After each inspection all available Officers of the Battalion were assembled for a short talk by the G.O.C. Division. At 10 p.m. report received at Brigade Hdqrs to the effect that a general strike was likely to occur the following day. On the strength of this information the Division placed one Company of the 5/6th Royal Scots and one Company 9th Battalion Machine Gun Corps at the disposal of this Brigade in case of necessity. In anticipation of the strike the Burgomaster was ordered to assemble the strike leaders at the Rathaus | |

Army Form C. 2118.

# WAR DIARY
## or
## INTELLIGENCE SUMMARY.
*(Erase heading not required.)*

Instructions regarding War Diaries and Intelligence Summaries are contained in F.S. Regs., Part II. and the Staff Manual respectively. Title pages will be prepared in manuscript.

| Place | Date | Hour | Summary of Events and Information | Remarks and references to Appendices |
|---|---|---|---|---|
| BENRATH. GERMANY. | 27/5/19 | | at 9 a.m. the following morning. One Company of the 4th Royal Scot Fusiliers was ordered to report at Benrath by 8.30 a.m. | |
| | 28/5/19 | | At an early hour information was received that a general strike had been proclaimed. At 9 a.m. the B.G.C. proceeded to the Rathaus to interview the strike leaders. After extracting from them that they had knowingly come out on strike in defiance of British Authority the B.G.C. placed eleven of the strike leaders under arrest, and despatched them under an escort to Cologne by lorry. The Company of the Royal Scot Fusiliers were disposed of as follows:- | |
| | | | 2 Platoons to the Deutsche Machine Fabrik. | |
| | | | 1 Platoon to the Electrical Power Works. | |
| | | | 1 Platoon to the Benrath Water Works. | |
| | | | The 8th Scottish Rifles were ordered to place a guard over the Hilden Waterworks. | |
| | | | At 10 a.m. the B.G.C. visited the Deutsche Machine Fabrik and assembled all the employees together and addressed them to the effect that as they had come out on strike in defiance of British Authority, their leaders in the first place had been arrested and he proposed to deport a percentage of the workers who refused to go back to their work. Ten arrests were made on the spot. | |
| | | | At 2 p.m. it was reported that a large assembly had gathered in front of the Rathaus in order to demand the release of their leaders. The O.C. 9th Scottish Rifles was ordered to verify this statement, and to disperse the crowd if necessary by using a Company of the 5/6th Royal Scots which had by this time arrived in Benrath. This statement was proved correct and the crowd was quickly dispersed by marching the Company 5/6th Royal Scots to the Rathaus. | |
| | | | At 4 p.m. a meeting was sanctioned to be held in front of the Rathaus in order that the men might be given a chance of being persuaded to go back to their work by a leader who was anxious to address the strikers on this policy. The result of this meeting was that by almost a unanimous vote the workers refused to resume work. Accordingly the B.G.C. issued the following proclamation. | |
| | | | "Until further orders the following restrictions are in force.- | |
| | | | 1. Restaurants, Cafes and Public Houses will be closed. | |

Army Form C. 2118.

# WAR DIARY
## *or*
# INTELLIGENCE SUMMARY.
*(Erase heading not required.)*

Instructions regarding War Diaries and Intelligence Summaries are contained in F. S. Regs., Part II. and the Staff Manual respectively. Title pages will be prepared in manuscript.

| Place | Date | Hour | Summary of Events and Information | Remarks and references to Appendices |
|---|---|---|---|---|
| BENRATH GERMANY. | 28/5/19 | | 2. Circulation in the streets is permitted between the hours of 6 a.m. and 6 p.m. Persons who wish to work may obtain special work passes to proceed to and from their work outside the above hours, on application to their respective factories, these passes will be issued by the Burgomaster. This order does not apply to Doctors, Mid-wives, Nurses or persons employed on Public Services who wear uniform or special badges of their office. Special work passes will be stamped by the Burgomaster and counter-signed daily by the employer, with the date and the time of arrival at the factory.<br><br>3. All meetings notified or sanctioned are cancelled. No meetings of any description will be permitted.<br><br>4. No congregation of persons or more than five in number is allowed, except in Places of Worship.<br><br>5. All lights with the exception of public lights will be extinguished by 10 p.m.<br><br>6. All night passes at present in circulation are cancelled."<br><br>No attempt was made to contravene these orders and at 6 p.m. there was hardly a person to be seen in the streets. As a precaution, however, the Machine Gun Company of the 9th Battalion Machine Gun Corps was ordered to mount their guns at various points in the centre of the town, and picquets were sent out to ensure that the orders were being carried out. During the night some 30 arrests were made of men who had been ear-marked as undesirables, and deported across the Holthausen Barrier into the Neutral Zone and their passes confiscated. | |

Army Form C. 2118.

# WAR DIARY
or
## INTELLIGENCE SUMMARY.
*(Erase heading not required.)*

Instructions regarding War Diaries and Intelligence Summaries are contained in F. S. Regs., Part II and the Staff Manual respectively. Title pages will be prepared in manuscript.

| Place | Date | Hour | Summary of Events and Information | Remarks and references to Appendices |
|---|---|---|---|---|
| BENRATH Germany. | 29/5/19. | | Being Ascension Day and therefore a General Holiday for the German people it was impossible to ascertain what was the true situation of the Strike. It appeared however, that opinion was divided and it seemed likely that work would generally be resumed on the Saturday. Nothing of interest occured during the day, but during the night 29/30th some further arrests were made of men for deportation. With the exception of 3 or 4 factories work was normally resumed. | |
| | 30/5/19. | | Nothing of interest occured during the day. Some 45 arrests were made in the HILDEN district on night 30/31st May, but were released as they wished in all cases to resume work on Monday. In view of the fact that the majority of workers had gone back to their work, the B.G.C. issued a second proclamation as follows:- "Work having been resumed by a large number of men I herewith give the following order :- 1. Estaminets, Cafes, etc are allowed to be open between the hours of 10.a.m. and 6.p.m. 2. Circulation of Civilians in the streets is permitted until 8.p.m. All other orders which have been issued on account of the Martial Law remain in force." At 11.p.m. information was received from a fairly reliable source that the Spartacists of DUSSELDORF intended raiding some post on the Perimeter with a view to sending Arms and Ammunition to the workers of BENRATH. One Section Machine Guns was sent by lorry to re-inforce each of the HOLTHAUSEN and HIMMELGEIST Posts, also the A/51st.Battery.R.F.A. were ordered to send single guns to each of the HOLTHAUSEN, HIMMELGEIST and FRIEDHOF Posts to prevent any on-rush that might have occured. Nothing however transpired during the night and the Machine Guns and Field Artillery returned to their Billets about 5.a.m. | |
| | 31/5/19. | | Church Parades. Nothing of interest occured. It appeared now that the Strike question had been completely settled and that it seemed likely that all factories would resume work on Monday. | |

31.5.19.

*[signature]* Brigadier Genrl.
Commanding 3rd.Lowland Brigade.

Lmr Div.
HQ 3rd Lmr Bde.

# WAR DIARY
or
## INTELLIGENCE SUMMARY.
*(Erase heading not required.)*

Army Form C. 2118.

Instructions regarding War Diaries and Intelligence Summaries are contained in F. S. Regs., Part II. and the Staff Manual respectively. Title pages will be prepared in manuscript.

| Place | Date | Hour | Summary of Events and Information | Remarks and references to Appendices |
|---|---|---|---|---|
| BENRATH | 1/6/19. | | All factories were reported to be in full working order on Monday morning both in the HILDEN and BENRATH district. The following proclamation was issued by the B. G. C.:- "Work having been resumed by a large number of men I herewith give the following order.:- Estaminets, Cafes, etc are allowed to be open between the hours of 10.a.m. and 6.p.m. Circulation of Civilians in the streets is permitted until 8.p.m. All other orders which have been issued on account of the Martial Law remain in force." The Company of the 5/6th Royal Scots were returned to their Battalion in the 2nd Brigade. The guard on the Deutsche Machine Fabrik was reduced to one platoon. | |
| | 2/6/19. | | All guards with the exception of the platoon at the Electrical Power Works were withdrawn. The following proclamation was issued by the B. G. C.:- "In view of the fact that the workers of the BENRATH and HILDEN area have complied with the British Military Orders, I hereby remove such restrictions as I have placed upon the Civilians of this area with the following exception No meeting of any kind whatever will be held in any place or building within this area until further orders. Any infringement of this order will be severely delt with." | |
| | 3/6/19. | | In order to celebrate the King's Birthday the day was proclaimed as a General Holiday with the exception of a short ceremonial parade of all available troops not on duty on the outpost lines at BENRATH and HILDEN at 12.00 Hours. In the afternoon a Garden Fete was held in the Schloss Grounds at Benrath, for which the Band of the 17th Lancers was obtained. The Programme for the afternoon consisted of various sports, including Mule Racing, and a concert-given by the Brigade Concert Party in the Gardens at 19.30 hours. Teas and suppers were provided for the men in the Schloss Gardens. The platoon at the Electrical Power Station was withdrawn. | |

Army Form C. 2118.

# WAR DIARY
## or
## INTELLIGENCE SUMMARY.
*(Erase heading not required.)*

Instructions regarding War Diaries and Intelligence Summaries are contained in F. S. Regs. Part II. and the Staff Manual respectively. Title pages will be prepared in manuscript.

| Place | Date | Hour | Summary of Events and Information | Remarks and references to Appendices |
|---|---|---|---|---|
| BENRATH. | 4/6/19. | | The Company of the 1/4th Royal Scots Fusiliers were sent to rejoin their Battalion at HILDEN. Training as usual. | |
| | 5/6/19. | | Training as usual. | |
| | 6/6/19. | | Training as usual. | |
| | 7/6/19. | | Training as usual. All restrictions as regards Officers and O.Rs not leaving the Brigade Area were removed. Wiring carried out. | |
| | 8/6/19. | | Church Parades. | |
| | 9/6/19. | | Whit-Monday, General Holiday. | |
| | 10/6/19. | | Training as usual. 3rd Lowland Brigade Order No.1, containing instructions in the event of a further advance, was issued. | |
| | 11/6/19. | | Training as usual. | |
| | 12/6/19. | | Training as usual. | |
| | 13/6/19. | | Training as usual. The C-in-C, (Sir William Robertson) visited BENRATH and inspected the A/51st Bde. R.F.A. He also visited the Brigade Bakery, Schloss Gardens, etc, and was informed of the arrangements being made for a Garden Fete to be held on the 14th and 15th. | |
| | 14/6/19. | | Training as usual. The Very Rev. Wallace Williamson, C.V.O., D.D., Dean of the Thistle (Chaplin to the King,) delivered an address at REALSCHULE, HILDEN. | |
| | 14/6/19. 15/6/19. | | A Gala Garden Fete was held in the Schloss Gardens, BENRATH. Sports, Mule Races, Competitions, etc, took place, The Band of the 17th Lancers, The American Expeditionery Force Jazz Band were present. Miss Lena Ashwell's Concert Party gave a performance on the 14th. Teas and dinners were served to Officers on the Lawn. Refreshments to O.Rs. were provided. | |

Army Form C. 2118.

# WAR DIARY
## or
## INTELLIGENCE SUMMARY.
(Erase heading not required.)

Instructions regarding War Diaries and Intelligence Summaries are contained in F.S. Regs., Part II. and the Staff Manual respectively. Title pages will be prepared in manuscript.

| Place | Date | Hour | Summary of Events and Information | Remarks and references to Appendices |
|---|---|---|---|---|
| BENRATH. | 15/6/19. | | Church Parade. | |
| | 16/6/19. | | Training as usual. | |
| | 17/6/19. | | Lecture given by Mr. EMERSON BROWN at REALSCHULE, HILDEN on the "United Task of the English Speaking Peoples." Information received that 'J' day would be on the 29th June. Further Instructions issued to Units in the event of a further advance taking place. Administrative Instructions No.1. was also issued. Advance Party of 3rd Highland Brigade reached BENRATH at Midday. | |
| | 18/6/19. | | Training as usual. Further Instructions issued to Units. Copies of Proclamations "Order of Proclamation" and Proclamation to facilitate the work of the Armies in the interest of the Civil Population, and Proclamation of the C-in-C issued, to Units of the 3rd Highland Brigade arrived and were billetted at BENRATH and HILDEN. | |
| | 19/6/19. | | Personnel of Brigade School returned to Units. Copies of the Proclamation sent to Units for posting up in further occupied territory in case a further advance takes place. Order to Civil Population. S.S. 775. S.S. 776. | |
| | 19/6/19. | | All perimeter posts were taken over by personnel of the 3rd Highland Brigade. Headquarters of the 3rd Highland Brigade were established at Bahnhof Hotel BENRATH by 19.00 hours. Information received that 'J' day was indefinitely postponed. This information was forwarded to all Units concerned. | |
| | 20/6/19. | | Instructions No.4. giving code for notifying 'J' day. | |
| | 21/6/19. | | Major M.C. MORGAN M.C. Brigade Major proceeded to Tenth Corps to take up duties as GSS.O.2. Major E.O. UNDERHILL M.C. assumed temporary duties until Major Bowen arrived from England. | |
| | 22/6/19. | | Church Parades. | |
| | 23/6/19. | | Information received that 'J' day would be 03.15 Hours on 24th. All preparations made accordingly & Instructions sent to all concerned under 3rd Lowland Brigade Order No.5. | |

Army Form C. 2118.

# WAR DIARY
## or
## INTELLIGENCE SUMMARY.
*(Erase heading not required.)*

Instructions regarding War Diaries and Intelligence Summaries are contained in F. S. Regs., Part II and the Staff Manual respectively. Title pages will be prepared in manuscript.

| Place | Date | Hour | Summary of Events and Information | Remarks and references to Appendices |
|---|---|---|---|---|
| BENRATH | 23/6/1919. | | Information received at 19.00 hours that The New German Government would unconditionally sign the Peace Terms. Confirmation of this received by wire at 22.15 hours. Units notified accordingly. | |
| | 24/6/19. | | Training as Usual. | |
| | 25/6/19. | | Major A.P.BOWEN M.C., K.S.L.I. assumed duties of Brigade Major, vice Major MORGAN M.C., Transferred to 10th Corps. Training as usual. The C-in-C (Sir William Robertson) paid a short visit to this area. | |
| | 26/6/19. | | Training as usual. Route March by the 1/8th Scottish Rifles, and were inspected by the B. G. C. and Brigade Major. | |
| | 27/6/19. | | Lieut.(Temp.Capt) E.H.SALTONSTALL. M.C., 1/8th Scottish Rifles. will officiate as Staff Captain to 3rd Lowland Brigade, vice Lieut (Temp.Capt.) L.J.A.WILL, M.C. "The Worcester Regt" who assumed duties at Southern Division as D.A.A.G. | |
| | 28/6/19. | | Peace Signed. Wire received from Lowland Division to that effect at 18.45 hours. and 'A' day will be 30th June. Units notified accordingly. The Lowland Divisional Ammunition Column Sports held at HAUS HORST. | |
| | 29/6/19. | | Church Parades. 1/8th Scottish Rifles Sports Meeting held at HILDEN. | |
| | 30/6/19. | | All Perimeter Posts were taken over by personnel of the 3rd Lowland Brigade from the 3rd Highland Brigade. Reliefs completed by 18.00 hours. | |

Brigadier General,
Commanding 3rd Lowland Brigade.

Army Form C. 2118.

# WAR DIARY
## or
## INTELLIGENCE SUMMARY.
*(Erase heading not required.)*

Instructions regarding War Diaries and Intelligence Summaries are contained in F. S. Regs. Part II and the Staff Manual respectively. Title pages will be prepared in manuscript.

| Place | Date | Hour | Summary of Events and Information | Remarks and references to Appendices |
|---|---|---|---|---|
| BENRATH | 1/6/19. | | All factories were reported to be in full working order on Monday morning both in the HILDEN and BENRATH district. The following proclamation was issued by the B. G. C.:- "Work having been resumed by a large number of men I herewith give the following order.:- Estaminets, Cafes, etc are allowed to be open between the hours of 10.a.m. and 6.p.m. Circulation of Civilians in the streets is permitted until 8.p.m. All other orders which have been issued on account of the Martial Law remain in force." The Company of the 5/6th Royal Scots were returned to their Battalion in the 2nd Brigade. The guard on the Deutsche Machine Fabrik was reduced to one platoon. | |
| | 2/6/19. | | All guards with the exception of the platoon at the Electrical Power Works were withdrawn. The following proclamation was issued by the P. G. C.:- "In view of the fact that the workers of the BENRATH and HILDEN area have complied with the British Military Orders. I hereby remove such restrictions as I have placed upon the Civilians of this area with the following exception No meeting of any kind whatever will be held in any place or building within this area until further orders. Any infringement of this order will be severely delt with." | |
| | 3/6/19. | | In order to celebrate the King's Birthday the day was proclamed as a General Holiday with the exception of a short ceremonial parade of all available troops not on duty on the outpost lines at BENRATH and HILDEN at 12.00 Hours. In the afternoon a Garden Fete was held in the Schloss Grounds at Benrath, for which the Band of the 17th Lancers was obtained. The programme for the afternoon consisted of various sports, including Mule Racing, and a concert given by the Brigade Concert Party in the Gardens at 19.30 hours. Teas and suppers were provided for the men in the Schloss Gardens. The platoon at the Electrical Power Station was withdrawn. | |

Army Form C. 2118.

# WAR DIARY
## or
## INTELLIGENCE SUMMARY.
(Erase heading not required.)

Instructions regarding War Diaries and Intelligence
Summaries are contained in F. S. Regs., Part II.
and the Staff Manual respectively. Title pages
will be prepared in manuscript.

| Place | Date | Hour | Summary of Events and Information | Remarks and references to Appendices |
|---|---|---|---|---|
| BENRATH. | 4/6/19. | | The Company of the 1/4th Royal Scots Fusiliers were sent to rejoin their Battalion at HILD N Training as usual. | |
| | 5/6/19. | | Training as usual. | |
| | 6/6/19. | | Training as usual. | |
| | 7/6/19. | | Training as usual. All restrictions as regards officers and O.Rs not leaving the Brigade Area were removed. Wiring carried out. | |
| | 8/6/19. | | Church Parades. | |
| | 9/6/19. | | Whit-Monday, General Holiday. | |
| | 10/6/19. | | Training as usual. 3rd Lowland Brigade Order No.1, containing instructions in the event of a further advance. was issued. | |
| | 11/6/19. | | Training as usual. | |
| | 12/6/19. | | Training as usual. | |
| | 13/6/19. | | Training as usual. The C-in-C. (Sir William Robertson) visited BENRATH and inspected the A/51st Bde. R.F.A. He also visited the Brigade Bakery, Schloss Gardens, etc, and was informed of the arrangements being made for a Garden Fete to be held on the 14th and 15th. | |
| | 14/6/19. | | Training as usual. The Very Rev. Wallace Williamson, C.V.O., D.D., Dean of the Thistle (Chaplain to the King.) delivered an address at REALSCHULE, HILDEN. | |
| | 14/6/19. 15/6/19. | | A Gala Garden Fete was held in the Schloss Gardens, BENRATH, Sports, Mule Races,Competitions, etc, took place. The Band of the 17th Lancers, The American Expeditionary Force Jazz Band were present. Miss Lena Ashwell's Concert Party gave a performance on the 14th. Teas and dinners were served to Officers on the Lawn. Refreshments to O.Rs. were provided. | |

Army Form C. 2118.

# WAR DIARY
## or
## INTELLIGENCE SUMMARY.

(Erase heading not required.)

Instructions regarding War Diaries and Intelligence Summaries are contained in F.S. Regs., Part II. and the Staff Manual respectively. Title pages will be prepared in manuscript.

| Place | Date | Hour | Summary of Events and Information | Remarks and references to Appendices |
|---|---|---|---|---|
| BENRATH. | 15/6/19. | | Church Parade. | |
| | 16/6/19. | | Training as usual. | |
| | 17/6/19. | | Lecture given by Mr. EMERSON BROWN at REALSCHULE, HILDEN on the "United Task of the English Speaking Peoples". Information received that 'j' day would be on the 23rd June. Further instructions issued to Units in the event of a further advance taking place. Administrative Instructions No1. was also issued. Advance Party of 3rd Highland Brigade reached BENRATH at Midday. Training as usual. | |
| | 18/6/19. | | Training as usual. Further instructions issued to Units. Copies of Proclamations "Order of facilitate the work of the Armies in the interest of the Civil Population", and Proclamation of the C-in-C issued to Units of the 3rd Highland Brigade arrived and were billeted at BENRATH and HILDEN. | |
| | 19/6/19. | | Personnel of Brigade School returned to Units. Copies of the Proclamation sent to Units for posting up in further occupied territory in case a further advance takes place. Order to Civil Population. S.S. 775. S.S. 776. All perimeter posts were taken over by personnel of the 3rd Highland Brigade. Headquarters of the 3rd Highland Brigade were established at Bahnhof Hotel, BENRATH by 19.00 hours. Information received that 'j' day was indefinitely postponed. This information was forwarded to all Units concerned. | |
| | 20/6/19. | | Instructions No.4. giving code for notifying 'j' day. | |
| | 21/6/19. | | Major M.C. MORGAN M.C. Brigade Major proceeded to Tenth Corps to take up duties as G.S.O.2. Major E.O. UNDERHILL M.C. assumed temporary duties until Major Bowen arrived from England. | |
| | 22/6/19. | | Church Parades. | |
| | 23/6/19. | | Information received that 'j' day would be 03.15 hours on 24th. All preparations made accordingly & instructions sent to all concerned under 3rd Lowland Brigade Order No.5. | |

Army Form C. 2118.

# WAR DIARY
*or*
# INTELLIGENCE SUMMARY.
*(Erase heading not required.)*

Instructions regarding War Diaries and Intelligence Summaries are contained in F. S. Regs., Part II. and the Staff Manual respectively. Title pages will be prepared in manuscript.

| Place | Date | Hour | Summary of Events and Information | Remarks and references to Appendices |
|---|---|---|---|---|
| BENRATH | 23/6/19. | | Information received at 19.00 hours that The New German Government would unconditionally sign the Peace Terms. Confirmation of this received by wire at 22.15 hours. Units notified accordingly. | |
| | 24/6/19. | | Training as usual. | |
| | 25/6/19. | | Major A. P. BOWEN M.C., K.S.L.I. assumed duties of Brigade Major, vice Major MORGAN M.C., Transferred to 10th Corps. Training as usual. The G-in-C (Sir William Robertson) paid a short visit to this area. | |
| | 26/6/19. | | Training as usual. Route March by the 1/8th Scottish Rifles, and were inspected by the B. G. C. and Brigade Major. | |
| | 27/6/19. | | Lieut.(Temp.Capt) E.M. LATTONSTALL, M.C., 1/8th Scottish Rifles. will officiate as Staff Captain to 3rd Lowland Brigade. vice Lieut (Temp.Capt.) Lt.A.F.INT. M.C. "The Worcester Regt" who assumed duties at Southern Division as D.A.A.G. | |
| | 28/6/19. | | Peace Signed. Wire received from Lowland Division to that effect at 18.45 hours. and 'A' day will be 30th June. Units notified accordingly. The Lowland Divisional Ammunition Column Sports held at HAUS HORST. | |
| | 29/6/19. | | Church Parades. 1/8th Scottish Rifles Sports Meeting held at HILDEN. | |
| | 30/6/19. | | All Perimeter Posts were taken over by personnel of the 3rd Lowland Brigade from the 3rd Highland Brigade. Reliefs completed by 18.00 hours. | |

E. Pinwill
Brigadier General
Commanding 3rd Lowland Brigade.

**SECRET**

Amendment No.1.  R.M.24/73.

To 3rd. Lowland Brigade Order No.1.   Copy.No...4....

Reference Map. Germany Sheet 59, 1/200,000; N.E.Europe 1/250,000 and Germany Sheet.2R. N.E.

1. Para.3.(d). delete and substitute:-

   "The area West of the GRAFRATH - VOHWINKEL - WALFRATH Road exclusive including the STADT GEMEINDES of SCHOLLER, GRUITEN, MILLRATH and ERKRATH".

2. Para.6.(b). Delete last line "to cover exits of DUSSELDORF" and substitute "to cover any portion of the New General Line of the Brigade".

3. Para.7. Original, Table "A" will be destroyed and attached table "A"1 will be substituted in its place.

4. Para.8.(e). Delete and substitute:-
   "Consequent on the alteration in moves, DUSSELDORF, ELLER, GLASSHUTTE, GERRESHEIM and METTMANN will now be taken over under the Belgian/French Administration in case of advance. The boundary between the British and Belgians will be as follows:-
   Present boundary from the Rhine as far as REISHOLZ Post inclusive, thence North along the DUSSELDORF GEMEINDE boundary to the stream East of GLASSHUTTE, thence along the stream to METTMANN exclusive, thence to NEVIGES inclusive and LANGENBURG exclusive".

5. The final areas to be occupied by the 1st and 2nd Lowland Brigades are as follows:-
   1st.Brigade.   BARMEN and the remainder of the Lowland Divisional Area to the East, including the GEMEINDES of BARMEN, SCHWELM, GERRESBERG, and NDR and OBR SBROCKHOVEL.

   2nd.Brigade.   From the GRAFRATH VOHWINKEL WALFRATH Road inclusive, Eastward to include the GEMEINDES of KRONENBURG, ELBERFELD, DONBURG and NEVIGES.

6. 3rd. Lowland Divisional Order No.1. will be amended accordingly.

   Acknowledge.

                                        M.C.Morgan   Major.
                                                     Brigade Major.
                                                     3rd. Lowland Brigade.
10/6/19.

Copies to :-
   All recipients of 3rd. Lowland Brigade Order No.1.
       dated 26/5/19.

SECRET.

Copy. No...4...

## 3rd. Lowland Brigade Order No.1.

Ref. 1/200,000 Map. and 1/250,000

1. In the event of the existing Armistice being terminated, hostilities will commence on "J" Day, after 72 hours warning.

    The Allies then advance to seize the RUHR BASIN, the German Railways essential for our advance, together with all rolling stock and German personnel for working the lines under our orders.

    The date of the probable "J" day will be communicated to all concerned and the exact hour and date of the advance notified subsequently.

2. The Railways of primary importance in the British Zone are:-
    (a) COLOGNE - OPLADEN - GRAFRATH - HAGEN - SCHWERTE - PADERBORN
    (b) UNNA - SOEST - LIPPSTADT.

3. The advance of the Lowland Division, operating in conjunction with the Southern Division on the Right and the Belgian Army on the Left, will be carried out in two stages :-

    First Day. ("J")

    (a). <u>The Southern Division.</u>    The Southern Division will occupy BARMEN, RONSDORF and REMSCHEID.

    (b). <u>1st. Lowland Brigade Group.</u>
        ELBERFELD, and points 291 and 303 and area E of the VOHWINKEL - VELBERT ROAD.

    (c). <u>2nd. Lowland Brigade Group.</u>
        Area S of the WALFRATH - METTMAN - DUSSELDORF ROAD between the GRAFRATH - VELBERT ROAD and the HILDEN - UNTERBACH - ERKRATH - HUBELERATH ROAD.

    (d). <u>3rd. Lowland Brigade Group.</u>
        DUSSELDORF inclusive of
        The area West of the GRAFRATH - ~~GERRESHEIM LUDENBURG~~ and GOLZHEIM.
        VOHWINKEL-WULFRATH Road exclusive including the STADT GEMEINDES of SCHOLLER, GRUITEN, MILLRATH and ERKRATH.

    Second Day (J+1)    No change.

    Third Day. (J+2)

    (a). <u>1st. Lowland Brigade Group.</u> RONSDORF, BARMEN and SCHWELM and area to the North as far as the LANGENBURG - HETTINGEN ROAD (exclusive)

    (b). <u>2nd. Lowland Brigade Group.</u>
        CRONENBERG - ELBERFELD and the area as far North as the WALFRATH LANGENBURG ROAD (exclusive).

    (c). <u>3rd. Lowland Brigade Group.</u>    No change.

4. The boundary between the Lowland Division and the Belgians is as follows :- DUSSELDORF (BRITISH) METTMAN (BELGIAN) and the METTMAN - WALFRATH - LANGENBURG - HETTINGEN - WITTEN - HORDE - UNNA Road (all inclusive to the BELGIANS).

4. Para.8.(e). Delete and substitute:-
"Consequent on the alteration in moves, DUSSELDORF, ELLER, J.GLASSHUTTE, GERRESHEIM and METTMANN will now be taken over under the Belgian/French Administration in case of advance. The boundary between the British and Belgians will be as follows:-
Present boundary from the Rhine as far as REISHOLZ Post inclusive, thence North along the DUSSELDORF GEMEINDE boundary to the stream East of GLASSHUTTE, thence along the stream to METTMANN exclusive, thence to NEVIGES inclusive and LANGENBURG exclusive".

-----2-----

5. The following Units will compose the 3rd.Lowland Brigade Group :-

        3rd.Lowland Brigade.Headquarters.
        1/4th.Ryl.Scots.Fusrs.
        1/8th.Sco.Rifles.
        9th.Sco.Rifles.
        3rd.Lowland (L) T.M.B.
        1.Section of 27th.Field Ambulance.
        1.Section of the 63rd.Field Coy.R.E.
        107th.Coy.Divisional Train.
        1.Field Battery 51st Brigade R.F.A.
        1.Coy. 9th.Battn.M.G.C.

6. Dependant on the general advance, the following moves and reliefs will take place prior to "J" day.

"J" - 3 day. Advance parties of Civil Administration 3rd.Highland Brigade arrive and take over by 18.00 hours on "J" - 2 day from the 3rd.Lowland Brigade, the area comprising : BENRATH, HILDEN, OHLIGS, HAAN.

"J" - 2 day. 3rd.Highland Brigade Group arrive by rail to BENRATH and to be accommodated in BENRATH (1.Battalion) HILDEN (1.Battalion) OHLIGS (1.Battalion).

"J" - 1.day.

(a). One Company 9th.Battalion M.G.C. moves from LANGENFELD to BENRATH and HILDEN; one section reporting to, and to be under the orders of O.C.1/4th.Ryl.Scots.Fusrs. and O.C.1/8th.Scottish Rifles respectively, remainder to O.C. 9th.Scottish Rifles.

(b). 1.Section 60 pounder Battery 63rd.Brigade.R.G.A. will take up positions in the vicinity of HILDEN (under orders of B.G.C. 3rd. Lowland Brigade) to cover any portion of the New General Line of the Brigade.

(c). All posts and guards in the Area BENRATH,HILDEN,OHLIGS,and HAAN will be relieved under arrangements to be made by 3rd.Lowland Brigade and 3rd.Highland Brigade respectively. As regards sub-para (a) above, O.C.M.G.Company will make arrangements direct with O.C. Battalions concerned as to where sections should report.

7. The advance of the 3rd.Lowland Brigade will be carried out in accordance with attached table "A".

8. (a). The nature and conditions under which the advance will be carried out are unknown, but Units will be prepared to fight to gain the objectives laid down.

(b). Railways, power stations, Telephone Exchanges, and water supply will be specially guarded. Special instructions on these points will be issued later.

(c). The policy to be adopted towards civilians and the holding of the new Perimeter, after the advance, will be notified later.

(d). Dress: - Fighting Order, with box respirator carried and 120 rounds S.A.A. per man.

(e). The boundary between the 3rd.Lowland Brigade and the 2nd Lowland Brigade will be the HILDEN-UNTERBACH-MORP-HUBBLERATH ROAD (inclusive to the 3rd.Lowland Brigade) the Perimeter boundary being the Water Tower in the vicinity of where the MORP-HUBBLERATH track joins the main METTMAN-DUSSELDORF ROAD.

-----3-----

9. Administrative Instructions are being issued separately.

10. Brigade Headquarters will probably move on "J"-day to the vicinity of GRAFENBURG.

Acknowledge.

H.A.Hill Capt.
Staff Kaptain
for Captain.
Brigade Major.
3rd.Lowland Brigade.

26/5/19.

Headquarters,3rd.Lowland Brigade.
Issued through Signals at 0900

Copies to :-

No.1. B.G.C.
" 2. File.
" 3.& 4. War Diary.
" 5. 1/4th.Ry.Scots.Fusrs.
" 6. 1/8th.Sco.Rifles.
" 7.     9th.Sco.Rifles.
" 8. 3rd.Lowland (L) T.M.B.
" 9. 107th.Coy.Divisional Train.
" 10. 27th.Field Ambulance.
" 11. 9th.Bn.M.G.C.
" 12.& 13. 51st.Brigade.R.F.A.
" 14. 63rd.Field Coy. R.E.
" 15.& 16. Lowland Division.
" 17. Staff Captain.
" 18. Staff Captain.(Civil Duties).
" 19. Provost Officer.
" 20. Brigade Signal Officer.
" 21. 2nd Lowland Bde
" 22. 3rd Highland Bde
" 23. Lowland Division D.A.
" 24  63rd R.G.A.

TABLE A.1. attached to amendment No.1 to 3rd. Lowland Bde. Order No.1.

| Serial No. | UNIT. | From. | Route. | Final Destination and Billets. | Remarks. |
|---|---|---|---|---|---|
| 1. | 1/4th. R.S.F. 1 Sect. D. Coy, M.G.C. | Hilden. | Millrath-Gruiten. | Stadtgemeinde of SCHOLLER. | 1st. Line Transport of Units will march in rear of Serial No.4 in the order given, unless notified to the contrary. |
| 2. | 1/8th. S.R. 1 Sect. D. Coy. M.G.C. | Hilden. | —do— | GRUITEN. | |
| 3. | "A" Batt. 51st. Bde. R.F.A. | Bonrath. | —do— | MILLRATH. | |
| 4. | 1 Sect. 63rd. Fld. Coy, R.E. | Bonrath. | —do— | MILLRATH. | |
| 5. | 9th. S.R. D. South.G.Corps. (less 2 Sects.) 3rd. Low. T.M.B. | Benrath. | Hilden-Untorbach. | ERKPATH. | |
| 6. | 1 Sect. 27th. Fld. Amb. | Hilden. | As per Serial No.3. | MILLRATH. | |
| 7. | 107th. Coy, Div. Train. | Hilden. | To be notified later. | | |
| 8. | 3rd. Lowland Bde. H.Q. | Henrath. | Hilden-Prills. | HOCHDAHL. | |

Copy No. 4.                                              SECRET.        B.M.24/163.

Appendix "P" to be attached to 3rd Lowland Brigade Order No 1.
of May 26th.

1. In the event of an advance taking place, the following reports and returns will be rendered to Brigade H.Q. by wire or D.R.

 (a). **Morning Situation Report** (Daily) by 05.30 hours.

 (b). **Evening Situation Report.** (Daily) by 14.30 hours.

The above to be rendered by Battalions and A/51st Bde. R.F.A. from 'J' day inclusive.

2. Location of Headquarters of Battalions, T.M.B., and other Units attached to the 3rd Lowland Brigade to be rendered to Brigade H.Q. on arrival at new destination on 'J' day. Any subsequent move will be reported at once.

The location should be given as follows:-

 Town.
 Name & number of street or house.
 Map Reference on The DUSSELDORF 1/25,000 map if shown.

3. **Intelligence Summaries and Reports.**

 (a). Priority wire giving Unit of any prisoners captured as soon after capture as possible.

 (b). Daily Intelligence Summaries from Battalions only are required for the period 20.00 hours to 20.00 hours. These will be forwarded as follows:-

  (i). For period 20.00 hours ) By D.R.L.S. so as to reach
    to 16.00 hours   ) Bde H.Q. by 16.30 hours.

  (ii). For period 16.00 hours ) By wire or telephone to reach
    to 20.00 hours.   ) Bde. H.Q. by 21.00 hours.

4. It is pointed out that these reports have to be rendered to the Division and similarly from Division to Corps etc., by certain times, and therefore Units are requested to submit these to this Headquarters punctually.

5. A Brigade report centre will be established at the HOCHDAHL Post Office at 7.a.m. on "J" day, where all reports should be sent pending the Brigade Office being established on arrival. Location of Bde.H.Q. will be notified to all concerned as soon as possible.

Acknowledge.

17/6/19.

              Major.
              Brigade Major.
              3rd. Lowland Brigade.

Copies to:-
No. 1. B.G.C.
"  2. File.
"  3. War Diary.
"  4. War Diary.
"  5. 1/4th. R.S.F.
"  6. 1/8th. Sco. Rifles.
"  7. 9th. Sco. Rifles.
"  8. 3rd. Lowland (L) T.M.B.
"  9. 107th. Divisional Train.
" 10. "B" Section
No. 11. "D" Coy. 9th. Bn. M.G.C.
"  12. and 13. 63rd. Field Coy. R.E.
"  13. Staff Captain.
"  14. Staff Captain. (C.D).
"  15. Provost Officer.
"  16. Bde Signal Officer.
"  17. A/51st. Bde. R.F.A.
"  18. 63rd. Bde. R.G.A.
"  19. Fld. Ambulance

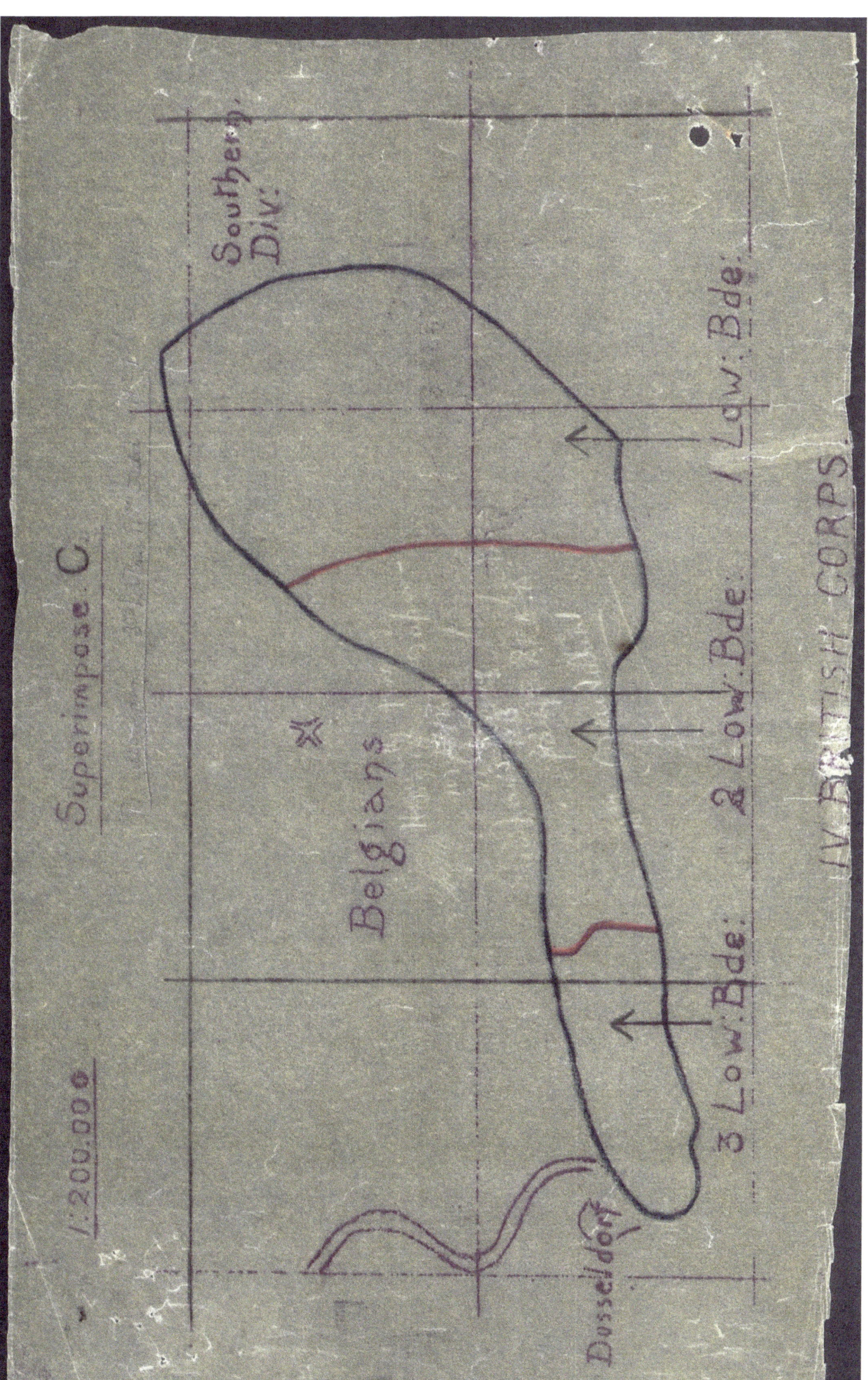

SECRET.   B.M.24/100.

Copy No. 4

### 3rd. Lowland Brigade Order No. 2.

Reference Map
DUSSELDORF
Sheet 4.
1/25,000

1. The Perimeter Posts and Guards now held by the 3rd. Lowland Brigade will be relieved tomorrow 19th June, by the 3rd. Highland Brigade.

2. The personnel employed at the REISHOLZ and HILDEN Stations Control, will remain, and will be handed over to the 3rd. Highland Brigade on "J" day.

3. The relief will be carried out in accordance with attached Table "A".

4. On completion of relief, the 1/4th.Ryl.Scots.Fusrs, and 1/8th.Scottish Rifles; will be concentrated in HILDEN in readiness for "J" day.

5. Completion of reliefs will be reported to Brigade H.Qrs.

6. All details of reliefs will be arranged between Commanding Officers concerned.

7. Acknowledge.

Issued to Signals at 20.00 hours.

M.C.Magau
Major.
Brigade Major,
3rd. Lowland Brigade.

18/6/19.

Copies to :-

No. 1. B.G.C.
" 2. Staff Captain.
" 3. War Diary.
" 4. ...do....
" 5. File.
" 6. 1/4th.R.S.F.
" 7. 1/8th.Sco.Rifles.
" 8. 9th.Sco.Rifles.
" 9. 3rd.Lowland (L) T.M.B.
" 10. Brigade Signal Officer.
" 11. 11th.Royal Scots.
" 12. 2nd.Lowland Brigade.
" 13. 3rd.Highland Brigade.
" 14. Lowland Division "G".
" 15. 5/6th.Royal Scots.
" 16. Provost Officer.
" 17. Staff Captain. (O.D)

TABLE "A" attached to 3rd Lowland Brigade Order No.2.

| Serial No. | Post or Guard. | Bn. now holding. | To be relieved by. | Present Strength. Off. | Present Strength. O.R. | Remarks. |
|---|---|---|---|---|---|---|
| 1. | GRUITEN. | 11th. Royal Scots. | 1/4th.Bn.Seaforth Hlghrs. | - | 9. | 11th.Ryl. Scots will send 2 guides per post to be relieved to report to Bn. H.Q.1/4 Seaforth Hlghrs A/M OHLIGS at 9 |
| 2. | Railway Stn.E.8307. | Do. | Do. | 1 | 12. | |
| 3. | E1P. | Do. | Do. | 1 | 22. | |
| 4. | MILLERTHOR. | Do. | Do. | 1 | 34. | |
| 5. | KEIPERDICK. | 1/2th. R.S.F. | 8th. Black Watch. | 1 | 35. | 4th.R.S.F. and 8th. S.R. will send two guides for each post to be relieved, to report to Bde. H.Q. BENRATH at 10th. inst. 2.P.M |
| 6. | DICKHAUS. | Do. | Do. | 1 | 25. | |
| 7. | FEISHOLZ. | Do. | Do. | 1 | 36. | |
| 8. | DAUSTEG. | Do. | Do. | 1 | 15. | |
| 9. | FREIDHOF. | Do. | Do. | 1 | 25. | |
| 10. | HOLTHAUSEN. | 1/5th. Scottish Rifles. | Do. | 5 | 84. | |
| 11. | HEILIGEIST. | Do. | Do. | 3 | 84. | |
| 12. | RHENANIA PETROL INSTALLATION. | Do. | Do. | 3 | 95. | |

(Continued.)

| Serial No. | Post or Guard. | Bn. now holding. | to be relieved by. | Present strength. | Remarks. |
|---|---|---|---|---|---|
| 13. | 2 Railway Bridges at OEFFEL-KUIJKEN K.49.57. | 5/6th. R. Scots. | 8th. Bn. Black Watch. | 1 Platoon. | Do. two guides. Guides 9 AM |
| 14. | Railway Bridges at:- K.64.91 K.96.71 K.85.70 | 11th. R. Scots. | Do. | 1 Platoon. | Do. two guides. |
| 15. | L.I.O.A. Hut. HAAR. | Do. | Do. | 5 men. | - |
| 16. | BRUCKEN HOTTEN BRUGGE HAAR. | 5/6th. Royal Scots. | Do. | 2 men. | 1 guide. Guides 9 AM - |

SECRET.

Copy No. 4

## 3rd Lowland Brigade Instructions No. 2.

One of the principal objectives of the first stage of the advance is to secure complete control of the German Railway systems that are considered essential for a further advance.

The Railways of primary importance British Zone are given in para 2.(a). 3rd Lowland Brigade Order No.1. of 26th May.

The essential measures to be taken by advancing troops in the first instance to secure complete control over these Railways are as follows:-

To occupy stations and important junctions, to prevent any destruction of material or the escape of personnel; to put up the notices of which copies will be provided; to occupy the head railway offices of the various German systems; to compel German personnel to remain at their posts, more especially the head managers and sub-managers of the systems; to stop all movements of trains until control of the general management has been taken over by the Sous Commission of the C.I.O.P.C.

The Sous Commission of the C.I.O.P.C. is arranging to send Railway Liaison Officers and Staffs to the principal centres. (ELBERFELD and HAGEN).

Once the Sous Commission has taken over steps will be taken to ensure that :-
(a). No railway working is interfered with, and no Railway Officials are molested or interfered with in their work.
   In the first instance, these Railway Officials will have no passes, but the Sous Commission will provide them as soon as practicable.

(b). No Railway telephones or Telegraphs are interfered with; they are vital to the continued working of the Railway.

(c) No Railway buildings or premises are commandeered or occupied without reference to Brigade H.Q.Rs.

Acknowledge.

17/6/19.

Major.
Brigade Major.
3rd. Lowland Brigade.

Copies to all recipients of Appendix "B" to 3rd. Lowland Brigade Order No.1.

## S E C R E T.

ADMINISTRATIVE INSTRUCTIONS NO.1. dated 17/8/19, para.4.

1. The 3RD. HIGHLAND BRIGADE will detrain at HILDEN and not as stated therein.

Approximate times of arrivals at HILDEN Station are as follows:-

| Serial No. | UNIT. | Time of Arrival. |
|---|---|---|
| 1. | H.Q. 3rd. Highland Brigade. Detachment of R.E. 4th. Seaforth Highlanders (less 1 Coy.) 3rd. Highland T.M.B. | 18.38 hours. |
| 2. | 8th. Royal Highlanders. 258th. Coy, R.A.S.C. | 19.38 hours. |
| 3. | 6th. Royal Highlanders (less 1 Coy.) | 20.23 hours. |
| 4. | 1 Coy, 4th. Seaforth Highrs. Bde. H.Q. Transport. 4th. Seaforth Highrs. Transport. T.M.B. Baggage. Baggage Wagons of 6th. and 8th. Royal Highlanders. | 22.28 hours. |
| 5. | 1 Coy, 8th. Royal Highrs. Transport 6th. Royal Highrs. " 8th. " " | 01.54 hours. |

2. Provost Officer will arrange for Traffic Control in the vicinity of HILDEN Station during the detrainment.
3. Each Unit of 3rd. Lowland Bde. will please arrange for a sufficient supply of hot water to be ready at the billets of the units which is relieving it, in order that tea may be made without delay for the troops of each Unit as it arrives.
4. Assist. Staff Captain, 3rd. HIGHLAND Bde, is arranging guides to meet units as they arrive.

Henry Barr
Captain,
Staff Captain,
3rd. LOWLAND INFANTRY BRIGADE.

Copy No.1. 1/4th. R.S.F.
2. 1/8th. S.R.
3. 9th. S.R.
4. T.M.Batty.
5. 83rd.Fld.Coy.R.E.
6. 107th. Coy.R.A.S.C.
7. Staff Captain, Civil Duties.
8. Provost Officer.
9. Bde. Signal Officer.
10. Bde.Q.M.S.
11. File.
(12 War Diary. )
(13
14. Ass. S.C.,3rd. Highland Bde.

SECRET.                                              Copy No. 20

## 3RD. LOWLAND INFANTRY BRIGADE.

ADMINISTRATIVE INSTRUCTIONS No.1.
(Issued in conjunction with 3rd. Lowland Infantry Brigade Orders
No.1. dated 26/5/19.)

Reference Maps,
1/200,000 and
1/250,000.

1. **DISPOSAL OF SURPLUS KIT.**

   (a) All surplus baggage, including one blanket per man, the second suit, crockery, mess property, recreational kit, educational books, rifles, box respirators, and steel helmets of personnel on leave which cannot be carried on the available transport, will be stored by units of 3rd. Lowland Infantry Brigade, at the REALSCHULE, HILDEN, by J-2 day in the accommodation which has already been allotted and indicated to Units by 1/4th. R.S.F.

   (b) Other Units of the Brigade Group will make their own arrangements as to the disposal of their surplus kit. If more accommodation is required in No.3. Sub.Area, application will be made at once to the Staff Captain, Civil Duties.

   (c) Each Unit will detail personnel not exceeding the following numbers to remain at the REALSCHULE, HILDEN, in charge of its stores:-

   Bde. H.Q. and Signals.   3 O.R.
   T.M. Battery.            1 O.R.
   Each Battalion           1 Officer, 1 N.C.O. 6 O.Rs.*

   * Includes 1 Storeman, per company, 1 representative of the Q.M. Stores, and 1 representative, Officers Mess.

   This personnel will be left with three complete days rations in hand.

2. **DISPOSAL OF AREA & REQUISITIONED STORES.**

   All stores which have been supplied by the German Civil Authorities on Requisition will be accounted for by Units as follows:-

   (a) <u>Plates, mugs, palliasses.</u>

   As there may be difficulty or delay in procuring plates, mugs, and palliasses, in the New Area:-
   (i) Plates and mugs will be dumped with the surplus stores at the REALSCHULE, HILDEN.
   (ii) Palliasses will be emptied out into one straw dump, to be selected by each unit in its present area, and then sent to the REALSCHULE, HILDEN.

   (b) <u>All other REQUISITIONED STORES.</u>

   All requisitioned stores other than plates, mugs, and palliasses will be collected into a Unit dump in the Area to be occupied by the relieving unit of the 3rd. Highland Infantry Brigade, by 14.00 hours on J-2 day.

   The relieving Unit may take over these stores, but failing its being able to do so before a move is ordered, the Staff Captain, Civil Duties, will instruct Burgermeisters, to take over these stores and grant receipts for them.

   In all cases where stores are handed over by a Unit, duplicate receipts will be taken and a copy forwarded to the Staff Captain, Civil Duties.

## 3. Battle Surplus.

No battle surplus will be left behind.

## 4. Relief by and Concentration of 3rd HIGHLAND INFANTRY BRIGADE in No 3.Sub-Area.

(a) The concentration of the 3rd.HIGHLAND INFANTRY BRIGADE in No.3.Sub-Area will be effected by means of Tactical Trains, the troops detraining at BENRATH Station on the afternoon of J-2 day being billetted as follows :-

| | |
|---|---|
| 3rd HIGHLAND INFANTRY BRIGADE H.Q. | BENRATH. |
| 6th ROYAL HIGHLANDERS. | HILDEN. |
| 8th  "         " | BENRATH. |
| 4th SEAFORTH  " | HILDEN. |
| 3rd HIGHLAND. (L) T.M.B. | BENRATH. |
| Detachment of R.E. | BENRATH. |
| Field Ambulance. | HILDEN. |
| Train of R.A.S.C. | HILDEN. |

(b) The Staff Captain, Civil Duties is issuing instructions with regard to the provision and allotment of billets to Units of that Brigade.

(c) All Billetting returns will be completed by Units on A.F.W.3856 and forwarded to the Staff Captain, Civil Duties on vacation of billets.

(d) Units will hand over Area duties such as the feeding of Railway Control Posts, Y.M.C.A. personnel, Church Army personnel, and the provision of Guards at HILDEN Station Refilling Point and the RATHAUS, BENRATH, to the 3rd. HIGHLAND INFANTRY BRIGADE by J-1 day.

## 5. Transport.

(a). Lorries.

Lorries for the transport of packs, one blanket per man (to be rolled in bundles of 10) and such stores as may be considered necessary, are allotted as follows:-

| | |
|---|---|
| Brigade H.Q. | 2. |
| Each Battn. | 2. |
| T.M.Batty. | 1. |

These lorries will report to the Headquarters of Units at 16.00 hours on J-1 day and will be sent back by Units to the Park at KRONPRINZ FACTORY, OHLIGS, after the first day's march.

(b). 1st Line and Train Vehicles.

(i). Baggage wagons will report to Units at ~~18.00 hours on J-1 day.~~ 1600 hours on J-2 day.

(ii). First Line Baggage wagons will march with and under the orders of Units concerned.
(iii). Supply wagons will march under orders of 107th Coy. R.A.S.C.

## 6. AMMUNITION.

(a) First Line Vehicles will carry the full authorised establishment of S.A.A. Grenades and Fireworks, as laid down in S.C.23/1493 dated 20/4/19.

(b) No Brigade Reserve of Ammunition will be formed.
In the event of Active Operations, Battalion First Line Reserves will be refilled from the S.A.A. Section, D.A.C. on application to the Staff Captain.
The S.A.A. Section moves to VOHWINKEL on J.day, and will deliver S.A.A. etc. to the First Line Transport of Units.
The Orderly delivering the application will be responsible for guiding the D.A.C. Limbers from Brigade H.Q. to the First Line Transport of the Unit concerned.

(c) One half of No.2. Section, D.A.C. will come under orders of 3rd. Lowland Infantry Brigade on J day for the purpose of feeding "A"/51st. BRIGADE, R.F.A.

## 7. SUPPLIES.

(a) From J. day inclusive, supplies will be delivered to Units by the Supply Section of the 107th. Coy, R.M.S.C., for consumption on the following day.

(b) Meeting point for guides will be notified later.
Iron Rations will be issued from Refilling Point on J-1 day to complete to the scale of 1 Iron Ration per man.
1/4th. R.S.F. will allot to the Brigade Supply Officer accommodation in the REALSCHULE, HILDEN to store any balance not issued.

## 8. WATER.

(a) Water Bottles and Water Carts will move full.

(b) 1 additional Water Cart complete with harness and one pair of L.D.H. will be issued to each Infantry Battalion, Battery, and Train Coy., for the advance.

## 9. MEDICAL.

(a) "B" Section, 27th. Field Ambulance, will be responsible for the evacuation of casualties and sick of the Brigade Group.

(b) One M.A.W. and detachment will accompany the 9th. Scottish Rifles, D. Coy, M.G.C., less 2 Sections and the T.M.B. on the Hilden-Unterbach-Road.

(c) The remainder of the Section will accompany the rest of the Brigade Group on the Hilden-Millrath-Gruiten-Road.

(d) Arrangements are being made for the Field Ambulance of the Highland Division, which is taking over at HILDEN, to clear the sick of this Area on J day at the usual hour from the Medical Inspection Rooms of Units.

(e) O.C. "B" Section, 27th. Fld. Ambulance is arranging to collect sick in M.A.W.s. from the H.Q. of each unit, on its arrival in the new billets.

## 10. BILLETS IN NEW AREA.

(a) Billets will be allotted in the new area in accordance with table A.1. of Order No.1., by 3rd. Low. Inf. Bde. H.Q. to all units of the Brigade Group. No billets are to be occupied without this authority.

(b) Billeting accommodation and the resources of the country are to be used primarily with a view to promoting the comfort and security of the troops.
The requirements of the inhabitants are to be met in a reasonable way after the requirements of the troops have been satisfied.
This ruling applies equally to the Occupied Territory during the preliminary concentration, prior to the advance.

---4---

(c). Care must be taken to ensure that the "Requisitioning Regulations" are strictly adhered to while on the move. For the first week, in a fixed Area, if all requests for Civil Services are sent to the Staff Captain, Civil Duties, in duplicate, one copy can be immediately passed for action and R.O. and R.O.R. can be passed later.

(d). The following billetting parties with bicycles or mounted will be detailed in advance and will march behind the leading Battalion of each Column :-

| | |
|---|---|
| Brigade Headquarters. | Staff Captain, Civil Duties. Camp Commandant, 4.O.R. a Provost Officer and 1 Interpreter. |
| T.M.Battery. | 1.Officer 2. O.R's. |
| Each Battalion. | 1.Officer 5. O.R's. |
| Each Battery. | 1.Officer 3. O.R's. |
| Mobile Section. ) 63rd.Field Coy.R.E. ) | 1.Officer. 2. O.R's. |
| "D" Coy.9th.Bn.M.G.C. | 1.Officer. 2.O.R's. |
| "B" Sect.Field Ambulance. | 1.Officer. 2.O.R's. |
| 107th.Coy.R.A.S.C. | 1.Officer. 2.O.R's. |
| ½ No.2. Sect.D.A.C. | 1.Officer. 2.O.R's. |

## 11. ORDNANCE

(a). D.......S.Stores are remaining at OHLIGS until the supply Railhead moves.
(b). A reserve of 500 box respirators and 250 containers; Machine Guns, Lewis Guns and Spare Parts is being maintained by D.A.D.O.S.

## 12. VETERINARY.

(a). No stable will be taken over or used in the New Area until it has been thoroughly disinfected under the direction of a Veterinary Officer. Until this has been done, all animals will be picketed in the open.

(b). No wooden water troughs, hay racks, or mangers will on any account be used. There is no objection to the use of those made of Iron provided that they have been thoroughly disinfected.

(c). Animals will not be watered from wells. Running streams are always preferable, buckets should be used until suitable troughs are available.

(d). No civilian forges will be used.
Animals must be shod in their own lines.

## 13. TRAFFIC CONTROL, etc.

(a). D.A.P.M., Lowland Division is making all necessary arrangements for Police and Traffic Control.

(b). Examining Posts are being established along the front on the main roads, no Civilians being allowed to pass whose papers are not in order.

(c). Provost Officer, and Police employed under him will move forward with Brigade H.Q.
He will arrange for copies of "ANORDUNG" to be posted up.

(d). The D.A.P.M., Lowland Division is arranging for routes to be properly marked and is erecting direction boards as the advance proceeds.

## 14. PERSONNEL AND RECEPTION CAMP.

Personnel returning from leave on "J" Day and subsequent days

Until the Personnel Railhead moves from OHLIGS, will be met at OHLIGS Station by the Details Officer of each Battalion referred to in para.1.(c) under arrangements to be made by them with the Commandant, Divisional Reception Camp and conducted to the REALSCHULE, HILDEN, where each will be issued with his rifle,120 rounds of S.A.A., box respirator and steel helmet.

For the purpose of sending up personnel to Units, the Commandant, Divisional Reception Camp, will have a direct call on the M.T. Coy, for Lorries.

All men proceeding on leave will leave their rifles,etc.,at their Units Store,REALSCHULE, HILDEN, prior to reporting to the Reception Camp.

## 15. CLOTHING AND BATHS.

Arrangements will be made by Units for all men who have not had baths and clean changes within the last four days to be bathed without fail during the next three days.

All dirty clothing must be returned to the Brigade Store, before 20.00 hours on J-2 days as the store has to be cleared to the Army Laundry early on J-1 day.

All stocks of clean underclothing of Units will be stored in the Brigade Dump at REALSCHULE, HILDEN on J-1 day.

## 16. DEMOBILIZATION AND CROSS POSTINGS.

Demobilization and cross postings in progress will continue.

## 17. PRISONERS OF WAR.

Divisional collecting Station for Prisoners and documents will be at GRAFRATH from J-3 day inclusive.

Acknowledge.

Captain,
Staff Captain.
3rd.Lowland Infantry Bde.

17/6/19.

Issued as Signals at 14-00 hours

Copy No. 1. 1/4th.R.S.F.
" 2. 1/8th.Sco.Rifles.
" 3. 9th.Sco.Rifles.
" 4. 3rd.Lowland (L) T.M.B.
" 5. Brigade School.
" 6. "D" Coy.9th.Bn.M.G.C.
" 7. A/51st.Bde.R.F.A.
" 8. 63rd Field Coy. R.E.
" 9. "B" Section 57th.Field Ambulance.
" 10. 107th.Coy.R.A.S.C.
" 11. Lowland Division.
" 12. Lowland Division "Q".
" 13. B.G.C.
" 14. Brigade Major.

Copy No. 15.Staff Captain.(C,D)
" 16.Provost Officer.
" 17.Bde.Signal Officer.
" 18.Camp Commandant.
" 19.File.
" 20.War Diary.
" 21. " do "
22. 2nd Low Bde
23. Bde Q.M.S

SECRET    Copy.No. 4

## 3rd. Lowland Brigade Instructions No. 1.

1. (a). Commencing on 'J' day 7th Squadron R.A.F. keeps one ~~Contract~~ Contact Machine and one Counter attack Patrol Machine on the front throughout each day.

   (b). 2 Special Reconnaissance Machines and 1 communication Machine stand by from 'J' day onwards.

   (c). Ground-Sheets will be displayed by Brigade H.Qrs. and Battalion H.Qrs. on arrival at respective destinations and ~~keep~~ Kept out until further orders.

2. No action will be taken on 'J' day until receipt of further definite orders.

2. HOSTAGES.

   It is possible that special I (b) officers may accompany Advance Guards for the purpose of seizing suspects in the area to be occupied.
   When demanded Units will supply guards.

4. Letter code calls will be issued to all concerned when received.

5. During the advance Red Very Lights (1") will be used by Infantry as a signal to indicate that the advance is being resisted by the enemy.

   Acknowledge.

                                    M.C. Morgan
                                    Major,
                                    Brigade Major,
                                    3rd Lowland Brigade.

17/6/19.

Copies to all recipients of appendix "B" to 3rd Lowland Brigade Orders No. 1.

SECRET  L.H.24/262.
Copy.No.

## 3rd.Lowland Brigade Order No.6.

Reference Map.
DUSSELDORF
Sheet.4.
1/25,000.

1. In the event of Orders being received for the return of Troops to their original Locations, Units will be prepared to carry out those moves on receipt of a message from 3rd.Lowland Brigade Headquarters.""A" day is ......."

2. On receipt of the above message the 1/4th.R.I.Scots.Fus. and 1/8th.Scottish Rifles. will take over the Perimeter Posts and Guards previously handed over by them to the 8th.Black Watch and now held by the 6th and 8th Black Watch.

3. All details of the relief to be arranged between Commanding Officers concerned. Reliefs to be completed by 18.00 hours on "A" day.

4. Completion of Reliefs will be reported to Brigade H.Qrs by 20.00 hours on "A" day.

5. Application ........ for trans if required will be made to the Staff Captain Civil Duties immediately on receipt of this order.

6. ACKNOWLEDGE.

Issued to Signals at. 17.30.

A.P.Bowe.

Major.
Brigade Major.
3rd.Lowland Brigade.

25/6/19.

Copies to all recipients of 3rd.Lowland Brigade Order No.2.of 10/6/19.

**SECRET.** B.M.34/201
Copy No. 4

## 3rd. Lowland Brigade. Instruction No. 3.

1. "J" day is indefinitely postponed, and in consequence no action will be taken tomorrow, nor will the present Perimeter be crossed until further definite orders are issued.

2. All Units will be ready to undertake the moves laid down on "J" day at short notice.

3. When the advance commences the policy as regards the use of Gas Shell and long range Artillery bombardment is:-

   In principle these means will only be employed against positions or places which have definitely been ascertained to be occupied by a hostile force, which is offering active resistance, or by an insurgent population.
   No gas shell, or H.E. is to be FIRED without sanction being obtained from Brigade Headquarters.

4. Acknowledge.

Issued to Signals at .17-30. hours.
19/6/19.

Copies to :-

| No. | |
|---|---|
| 1. | R.O.C. |
| 2. | File. |
| 3. | War Diary. |
| 4. | ...do... |
| 5. | 1/6th. Ryl. Scots. Fusrs. |
| 6. | 1/6th. Sco. Rifles. |
| 7. | 9th. Sco. Rifles. |
| 8. | 3rd. Lowland (D) T.M.B. |
| 9. | 107th. Coy. Divisional Train. |
| 10. | 57th. Field Ambulance ("B" Section). |
| 11. | "D" Coy. 8th. Bn. M.G.C. |
| 12.) | A/51st. Brigade. R.F.A. |
| 13.) | 5" B" R.A.A |
| 14. | 63rd. Field Coy. R.E. |
| 15.) | Lowland Division. |
| 16.) | |
| 17. | Staff Captain. |
| 18. | Satff Captain (O.D). |
| 19. | Provost Officer. |
| 20. | Brigade Signal Officer. |
| 21. | 2nd. Lowland Brigade. |
| 22. | 3rd. Highland Brigade. |
| 23. | Lowland Div. Artillery. |
| 24. | 63rd. Brigade R.G.A. |
| 25. | "A" Section 119. Battery R.G.A.(attached to 2nd Low Bde) |

M. Hagan
Major.
Brigade Major.
3rd. Lowland Brigade.

Sent to Formations and Units other than in 3rd Low Bde group by ordinary D.R.

Copy No. 4 …

SECRET.

B.M.24/210.

## 3rd LOWLAND BRIGADE INSTRUCTION NO. 4.

1. **NOTIFICATION OF "J" DAY.**

   In notifying "J" day the following code will be employed :-

   June 21st. = "A"
   June 22nd. = "B"
   June 23rd. = "C"
   June 24th. = "D"
   etc        etc.

   Thus if "J" day be June 24th, the following telegram would be sent to all Units of the 3rd Lowland Bde Group:-
   "Reference instructions No 4 "J" day equals "D" aaa. Acknowledge."

2. Infantry, and First Line Transport, march tables to starting points are attached :   As soon as it is known what time the Brigade is ordered to cross the perimeter, a wire will be sent to all concerned, e.g,
   "Reference instructions No 4 zero time 05.50 aaa. Acknowledge."
   This wire may be embodied in the "J" day code wire above.

3. **COMMUNICATIONS.**

   As the Telegraph and Telephone Communication is uncertain in the new Area, no reliance can be made on them for at least 24 hours : consequently Units must arrange for an adequate runner and cyclist service.
   One Motor Cyclist will report to Lieut Col. J.M.FINDLAY D.S.O. 1/8th Scottish Rifles, in command of the right column, at Zero hour - 30 minutes and will be at his disposal until the destination of the march is reached.

4. Brigade Headquarters will close at BENRATH and re-open at HOCHDAHL at times to be notified later.
   Reports to Brigade after the time of re-opening at HOCHDAHL will be delivered at the Post Office there.

5. Acknowledge.

   *H.C. Morgan*
   Major.
   Brigade Major.
   3rd Lowland Infantry Bde.

20/6/19.

Issued through Signals at 1200

Copies to all recipients of 3rd Lowland Brigade Order No 1 of 26th May.

## 1st LINE TRANSPORT and BAGGAGE WAGONS

### MARCH TIME TABLE Attached to 3rd Lowland Bde. Order No 1. of 29th Dec.

| Serial No. | Units | Starting Points | Time | Route | Remarks |
|---|---|---|---|---|---|
| 1. | 1/4th R.S.F. | As for Infantry. | Zero + 35 Mins. | As for Infantry | Transport Officer 1/4th R.S.F. will be in command of column until such time as Transport arrives at destination. |
| 2. | 1/8th S.R. | | Zero + 70 Mins. | | |
| 3. | C Batty 51st Bde R.F.A. | | Zero + 75 Mins. | | |
| 4. | 1 Sect. 63rd Fd. Coy. R.E. | | Zero + 80 Mins. | | |
| 5. | 1 Sect. Fd. Amb. | | Zero + 82 Mins. | | |
| 6. | 9th S.R. | As for Battn. | Zero hour | | |

Ref. Map DUSSELDORF
1/25,000 Sheet No.4.

## MARCH TABLE
### INFANTRY & ARTILLERY.

Attached to 3rd. Lowland Brigade Order No.4 of 7th May.

| Serial No. | UNIT. | Starting Point. | Time. | Route to S.P. | Remarks. |
|---|---|---|---|---|---|
| 1. | 1/5th. Ryl. Scot. Fusiliers. 1 Scot. D. Coy. M.G.C. | KLEF (road junct. at) K. 45.c2. | Zero hour. | ------- | Advance (Guard of 2 Coys. R.S.F. plus 1 Scot. M.G.C. under Major J.A.McEwen R.S.F. will pass S.P. at Zero — 50 mins. |
| 2. | 1/8th. Sco. Rifles. 1 Scot. D. Coy. M.G.C. | —Do— | Zero + 3 mins. | ------- | Column will be under Command of Lt.Col. J.R. Findley, D.S.O. 1/8th. Sco. Rifs., until such times as units arrive at their destination. |
| 3. | A. Batty. 51st. Bde. R.F.A. | —Do— | Zero + 12 mins. | HILDEN main Street as far as X Roads K.44-59 thence HIEF Road. | |
| 4. | 1 Sect. 83rd. Fd. Coy. R.E. | —Do— | Zero + 18 mins. | | |
| 5. | 1 Sect. 27th. Fd. Amb. | —Do— | Zero + 50 mins. | | |
| 6. | Brigade H.Q. | —Do— | Zero + 60 mins. | —Do— | Transport will be taken. |
| 7. | 107th. Coy. Div. Train. | —Do— | Zero + 85 mins. | —Do— | Destination HILDEN Sth. |
| 8. | 9th. Sco. Rifles. D. Coy, M.G.C. (less 2 Scots.) 3rd. Lowland (L) F.H.B. | BENRATH Station. | Zero — 50 mins. | ------- | O.C. 9th. Sco. Rifles. will be responsible for local protection. |

SECRET.

B.M.24/241.  Copy No. 3......

## 3rd. Lowland Brigade. Order No. 5.

1. All preparations will be made to commence moves laid down for "J" day at 03.15.hours (Zero hour) on 24th June.

2. No troops will cross the Perimeter until receipt of the following Urgent Operations Priority message:-"CROSS PERIMETER ZERO HOUR 24th AAA. ACKNOWLEDGE".
   Possibly this message may not be sent from D.H.Q., before 22.00.hours on 23rd.
   From noon onwards to-day an Officer must be in the office of each Unit.

3. As soon as troops of the Lowland Division have passed the Perimeter Posts Units of the Highland Division will be withdrawn and concentrated.

4. Contact aeroplanes of the 7th Squadron R.A.F. will fly a Yellow and Red streamer from their tails and will also carry black flaps attached to the rear edge of the lower plane, one on each side of the body.

5. Div. Report Centre will open N. of GRAFRATH at 04.00.hours on 24th.

6. ALL OFFICERS ARE TO BE WARNED THAT THEY ARE NOT TO LEAVE THEIR UNITS TO-DAY.

7. Acknowledge.

Issued to Signals at .14.00.hours.

[signature]   Major.
              Brigade Major.
23/6/19.      3rd. Lowland Brigade.

Copies to all recipients of 3rd. Lowland Brigade Order No.1, of 26th. May.

Army Form C. 2118.

# WAR DIARY
## or
## INTELLIGENCE-SUMMARY.
*(Erase heading not required.)*

Instructions regarding War Diaries and Intelligence Summaries are contained in F.S. Regs., Part II. and the Staff Manual respectively. Title pages will be prepared in manuscript.

| Place | Date | Hour | Summary of Events and Information | Remarks and references to Appendices |
|---|---|---|---|---|
| BENRATH. | 1/7/19. | | 3rd Highland Brigade returned to their usual location, left BENRATH and HILDEN at 13.00 Hours. Sports Meeting at Divisional College, at 15.00 hours all Units to send a representative. | |
| | 2/7/19. | | Training as usual. | |
| | 3/7/19. | | Training as usual. | |
| | 4/7/19. | | General Holiday. All Units arranged for sports for their men. Cricket Match between 3rd Lowland Brigade Group and 9th Bn. M.G.C. at HAUS HORST, BENRATH. Wire received from Division at 22.30 hours that Division was moving and the 3rd Brigade moves on the 7th inst to BEDBURG. | |
| | 5/7/19. | | Instructions sent out for advance parties at 22.45 hours. Wire received at 23.00 hours from Division that the move was postponed for 24 hours. Units were notified accordingly. A Grand Allied Bands Festival was held in the Schloss Gardens, BENRATH during the week-end, Sports, Mule Races, Indian Wrestling, Tug-of-War took place. Teas were served to Officers and N.C.O's. Refreshments were provided for O.R's. A Souper Dansant was held at night in the new Dancing Hall in the Schloss. | |
| | 6/7/19. | | Church Parades. United Service of Thanksgiving for Peace was held. | |
| | 7/7/19. | | Advance Parties left BENRATH for BEDBURG, at 10.00 hours. | |
| BEDBURG | 8/7/19. | | 3rd Lowland Brigade Group proceeded to BEDBURG, arrived at BEDBURG at 14.00 hours. Completion of reliefs at 18.00 hours. | |
| | 9/7/19. | | Training as usual. | |
| | 10/7/19. | | Training as usual. | |
| | 11/7/19. | | Training as usual. | |
| | 12/7/19. | | Lieut. T/Capt. E.R. SALTONSTALL, M.C., 1/8th Sco. Rifles, acting Staff Captain is appointed Staff Captain 3rd Lowland Brigade vice Lieut. T/Capt L.J.A.WILL, M.C. tobe D.A.A.G. Southern Division. Authy.Rhine Army A.734/45.M. dated 8/7/19. | |

Army Form C. 2118.

# WAR DIARY
## or
## INTELLIGENCE-SUMMARY.
*(Erase heading not required.)*

Instructions regarding War Diaries and Intelligence Summaries are contained in F. S. Regs., Part II. and the Staff Manual respectively. Title pages will be prepared in manuscript.

| Place | Date | Hour | Summary of Events and Information | Remarks and references to Appendices |
|---|---|---|---|---|
| BEDBURG. | 13/7/19. | | Church Parades.  9th Sco. Rifles moved from their camp at BEDBURG to NEURATH. | |
| | 14/7/19. | | Lieut. T/Capt. E.R. SALTONSTALL, M.C. proceeded to U.K. for 28 days leave Capt. H.E.C. BACON, M.C. 9th Sco. Rifles. assumed Temporary Appointment of Staff Captain vice Capt. SALTONSTALL. | |
| | 15/7/19. | | Riding Classes formed for Officers every Mondays, Wednesdays, & Fridays. under Lieut. G.E. POTTER, M.C., 7th Queens Own Hussars. | |
| | 16/7/19. | | Training as usual. | |
| | 17/7/19. | | Corps Commander came to see the B.G.C. and Battalion Commanders. | |
| | 18/7/19. | | Training as usual. | |
| | 19/7/19. | | General Holiday. Representatives of this Brigade took part in the "VICTORY PARIS MARCH". Sports and Smoking concerts were held by Battalions. | |
| | 20/7/19. | | Church Parades. | |
| | 21/7/19. | | B.G.C. and Brigade Major, inspected the Transport Turn-out of each Battalion for a competition to be held at Division. The 1/4th R.S.F. football team and competitors for the Belgian Sports left BEDBURG at 09.00 hours for NEUSS. The 1/4th R.S.F. Football Team represented the Brigade and played the Belgian Army of Occupation. Result. 1/4th R.S.F. 2 goals Belgian Army Nil. | |
| | 22/7/19. | | Training as usual. | |
| | 23/7/19. | | Training as usual. | |
| | 24/7/19. | | B.G.C. & Brigade Major visited KONIGSHOVEN where Major General TUDOR, C.B., C.M.G., inspected 1/8th Scottish Rifles Transport Turn-out for competition for the best Turn-out in the Division. | |

Army Form C. 2118.

# WAR DIARY or INTELLIGENCE SUMMARY

(Erase heading not required.)

Instructions regarding War Diaries and Intelligence Summaries are contained in F. S. Regs., Part II. and the Staff Manual respectively. Title pages will be prepared in manuscript.

| Place | Date | Hour | Summary of Events and Information | Remarks and references to Appendices |
|---|---|---|---|---|
| BEDBURG. | 25/7/19. | | Lecture by Major Wade on War Saving Certificates at Y.M.C.A., BEDBURG, for all troops in this area. | |
| | 26/7/19. | | Lecture by Major Wade on War Saving Certificates at KONIGSHOVEN for 1/8th S.R. and at NEURATH for 9th S.R. | |
| | 27/7/19. | | Battalion Sports of 1/8th S.R. at KONIGSHOVEN. Church Parades. | |
| | 28/7/19. | | Training as usual. A Lecture was given by Major A.P.BOWEN M.C. (B.M.) at Y.M.C.A. Hall BEDBURG on the "NAVAL RAID ON ZEEBRUGGE". | |
| | 29/7/19. | | C-in-C (general Sir W.R.ROBERTSON, G.C.B., K.C.V.O., D.S.O., A.D.C.) visited this area as follows - NEURATH 10.00 hours. to inspect 9th S.R. billets, BUCHHOLZ, 63rd Field Coy R.E. 10.45 hrs. BEDBURG 11.15 hrs. to inspect parade and billets of the 1/4th R.S.F. in SCHLOSS. | |
| | 30/7/19. | | Battalion Sports of 1/4th R.S.F. | |
| | 31/7/19. | | Training as usual. | |

Osborne maj—
Lieut. Colonel.,
Comdg. 3rd Lowland Infy. Bde.

S.C/00/169

### 3rd. Lowland Infantry Brigade.   SECRET.

1. Advance Parties will be detailed by each Unit mentioned below, to proceed to new Area tomorrow (6th. inst.) An officer will be sent with each party with the exception of Bde. Hqrs. to BEDBURG.

2. 2 Lorries will be provided for the journey. Advance parties of Units in Hilden Area will concentrate at the Headquarters, 1/8th. Scottish Rifles, Hilden, at 10.15 hours. One lorry will report there at that time to bring this party to Bde. H.Q. to join the Ronrath Party. Advance Parties of Units in Ronrath will report at Bde. H.Q. at 10.30 hours.

3. O.C. 1/8th. Scottish Rifles will detail a Captain to be in charge of the entire party; he will report immediately on arrival to the Staff Captain, 3rd. Light Brigade, BEDBURG.
   Complete kit, including blankets, and rations for Monday will be carried. These advance parties will take over all stores, requisitioned articles, etc., in the new area. A copy of all stores taken over will be forwarded to Brigade H.Q. on Tuesday, 8th. inst. Advance Parties will be accommodated by Units of the 3rd. Light Bde.

ACKNOWLEDGE.

Issued at Signals 22.45 hours.

5/9/19.

                                     Major,
                             Brigade Major,
           3rd. Lowland Inf. Brigade.

1/4th. R.S.F.
1/8th. S.R.
9th. S.R.
3rd. Low. T.M.B.
63rd. F.C. Coy, R.E.
107th. Coy, R.A.S.C.
Bde. Q.M.S.

SECRET.　　　　　　　　　Copy No. 3

## 3rd. Lowland Infantry Brigade.

Administrative Instructions No. 1.

(Issued in conjunction with 3rd. Lowland Bde. Orders No.1 dated 6/7/19.)

Ref. Maps. 59.
1/250,000.

1. **Advance Parties.**

   Advance Parties will proceed to new area tomorrow 7th. inst. by lorry as per orders issued separately.

2. **Trains.**

   Units will move in accordance with attached Table A.

3. **Supplies.**

   Troops moving by train will entrain with the current day's ration on the man or in cookers. Rations for the 9th. and following days will be delivered by lorry in the New Area. Units will commence drawing by horse transport on Friday, 11th.

4. **Lorries.**

   Lorries to carry stores are reporting to Unit Hqrs. as under on 7th. inst. These lorries will be instructed by Units to report loaded at Benrath Station at 08.00 hours on 8th. inst., and will proceed as a convoy. O.C. 1/8th. Scottish Rifles will detail 1 Officer to be in charge of the convoy and to proceed to BEDBURG with it:-

   | | | |
   |---|---|---|
   | Bde. H.Q. & T.M.B. | 2. | )
   | 1/4th. R.S.F. | 2. | )
   | 1/8th. S.R. | 2. | )
   | 9th. S.R. | 2. | ) 19.00 hours.
   | 63rd. Fld. Coy, R.E. | 1. | )
   | 107th. Coy, R.A.S.C. | 1. | )

5. **Prisoners.**

   Units will take over their prisoners at present under the charge of the D.A.P.M. and will retain them until accommodation is provided in the New Area.
   These men will be taken over tomorrow.

6. The following personnel of this Brigade will remain at their present duties until further orders:-

   Civil Administrative Staff.
   Hilden Station Control.
   Reisholz Station Control.

   Rations for 3 days will be left with them, after which they will be rationed by No. 4 Company R.A.S.C. Light Division.

7. Receipts for all tonnage will be taken and given in duplicate, one copy of receipt will be forwarded to Bde. H.Q. immediately on completion of move.

## 8. Transport.

The following transport will move by road on 8th. crossing the ferry at HIMMELGEIST. Thence via DORMAGEN-ROMMERSKIRCHEN-BERGHEIM-BEDBURG.

All Lewis Guns and S.A. Limbers of- 1/4th. R.S.F.
1/8th. S.R.
9th. S.R.

This transport will concentrate at 06.00 hours on 8th. inst. at Tram Terminus, Benrath.
Rations for 8th. and 9th. will be taken and if necessary the column will stage the night of 8th/9th.
O.C. 9th. S.R. will detail an officer to be in charge, he will report on arrival at BEDBURG to Bde. Hqrs.

## 9. Stores.

All requisitioned stores will be left in Situ, receipts will be obtained in duplicate and a copy sent to Bde. Hqrs. on arrival in New Area.

## 10. Entraining Officer.

Capt. Bacon, M.C., 9th. Scottish Rifles will be the Bde. Entraining Officer; he will entrain the whole of the Bde. personnel.
A copy of Entraining states will be given him by each unit on arrival at the station. He will travel on the last personnel train to Bedburg.

## 11. Loading Party.

O.C. 1/4th. R.S.F. will detail one complete company as loading party to report to Capt. Bacon, at Hilden Station at 06.00 hours, on 8th. inst., to load baggage and stores, being taken on personnel trains. When this is completed they will report to Transport Officer, 9th. Scottish Rifles, who will be Entraining Officer, for the whole Brigade Transport; and load transport on the Omnibus Trains.
Half this company will proceed on the first Omnibus train as unloading party for that train, the other half will travel with the last of the transport and unload that.

12. O.C. 9th. Scottish Rifles will detail a party of 1 Officer and 50 O.R's. to unload baggage from 1st. Personel Train, and O.C. 1/8th. S.R. a similar party to unload the second train.

13. Bde. Hqrs. will close at Benrath at 14.00 hours on 8th. and re-open at BEDBURG at the same hour.

ACKNOWLEDGE.

6/7/19.

*E R Saltonstall*
Captain,
Staff Captain,
3rd. Lowland Inf. Brigade.

Issued to Signals at 19-30.
Copies to:-
1. B.G.C.
2. File.
3. War Diary.
4.  "   "
5. 1/4th. R.S.F.
6. 1/8th. S.R.
7. 9th. S.R.
8. 3rd. Low. T.M.B.
9. 63rd. Fld. Coy, R.E.
10. 107th. Coy, R.A.S.C.
11. Bde. Signalling Officer.
12. Low. Division "G"
13. Low.    "    "Q"
14. Staff Captain,
15.   "      "    (Civil Duties.)
16. Provost Officer.
17. 3rd. Light Brigade.

3rd. Lowland Brigade.

## TABLE A.

| 1. Serial No. | 2. Date. | 3. Unit. | 4. Type of train. | 5. Entrain. | 6. Depart. | 7. Detrain. | DESTINATION. |
|---|---|---|---|---|---|---|---|
| 1. | July, 8th. | 1/4th. R.S.F. less 1 Coy. 9th. S.R. | Personnel. | Hilden. | 08.00. | BEDBURGH. | 1/4th.R.S.F. to Bedburgh. 9th. S.R. " " Camp |
| 2. | " 8th. | 3rd. Low. Bde. H.Q. 1/6th. S.R. 65rd. Fld. Coy, R.E. 107th. Coy, R.A.S.C. 3rd. Low. T.M.B. Bde. School. | " | " | 08.30. | BEDBURGH. | 3rd. Low. H.Q. Bedburg. 1/6th. S.R. to Konigshoven. 65rd. Fld.Coy.R.E. to Buchholz. 107th. Coy,R.A.S.C. to Morichen. T.M.B. à Bde.School.Personnel, Hillendorf. |
| 3. | " 8th. | Transport of 3rd. Low. Bde. H.Q. 1/4th. R.S.F. 1/6th. S.R. ½ Coy. 1/4th. R.S.F. | Omnibus. | " | 10.00. | ROHEERSKIRCHEN. | |
| 4. | " 8th. | 9th. S.R. 65rd. Fld.Coy,R.E. 107th.Coy,R.A.S.C. ½ Coy,1/4th. R.S.F. | " | " | 15.00. | ROHEERSKIRCHEN. | |

1. Train journeys will be about 4 hours.
2. Personnel Trains consist of 48 carriages and 2 officers' carriages ------ accommodated for 1000 all ranks. Omnibus Trains ......, 1 coach, 50 covers and 17 flats.
6 heavy draft, or 8 other animals, or 30 men go to a cover.
4. The average flat takes 4 axles.
5. In all cases, personnel will be at the Station 1 hour, and transport or baggage, 5 hours before time of departure.

3rd. Lowland Brigade.     Secret.     D.M. 24/352.
Order No. 1.              Copy No. 3

Reference Map 59
         1/250,000.

1. The 3rd. Lowland Brigade Group will be relieved by the 3rd. Light Brigade Group.
   Relief to be completed by 19.00 hours, July, 8th.

2. Moves will be carried out in accordance with Time Table issued with Administrative Instructions.

3. The relief of the Perimeter Posts and the guards at the Petrol Factory and Bde. H.Q. will be carried out as follows:-
   3 Companys of the 3rd. Light Brigade, arrive at 3rd. Lowland Brigade H.Q. at 13.00 hours, 8th. inst., by lorry.
   One Officer guide for each of the Posts and one for the Petrol Factory will be detailed by the Officer Commanding the Battalion furnishing the garrison of the post to report to the Bde. Major at 3rd. Lowland Brigade H.Q., Bonrath, at 12.30 hours, 8th. inst. These officers will guide the relieving garrisons to their respective posts.
   The O.C. 9th. Scottish Rifles will be detail 1 N.C.O. guide to take 3 men of the Light Brigade to relieve the 3 men of this Bde., at the Rifle Range, URDENBACH.
   This N.C.O. will report to Bde. Major at 3rd. Low. Bde. H.Q., at 12.30 hours, 8th. inst.
   Arrangements for the move of these garrisons when relieved will be notified as soon as possible.
   The Guard at 3rd. Lowland Bde. Hqrs. Mess will march out with the personnel of Bde. H.Q.

4. Civil Administration Staff remain in the present area with the Light Bde., for one week.

5. Maps, defence schemes, details of Civil Administration, training facilities, education and recreation, orders and regulations re Perimeter Post will be handed to relieving units of the Light Bde., Group.

6. All goods requisitioned in the present Lowland Bde. Area will be left in situ.

7. Completion of reliefs of Perimeter Posts and Guards and completion of moves on 8th. inst., will be wired to Bde. H.Q.

8. Railhead will be BEDBURG for 10th. July.

9. The 3rd. Lowland Brigade H.Q. closes at Bonrath and opens at BEDBURG at 14.00 hours on 8th. inst.

10. Units of the Light Division, moving into the Lowland Division Area and vice versa come under the command of the Lowland and Light Division respectively until 16.00 hours, July, 10th.

11. ACKNOWLEDGE.

                              Major,
                              Brigade Major,
6/7/19.                       3rd. Lowland Brigade.

Issued to Signals at  10-35
Copies to :-
1. B.G.C.                9. 3rd. Low. T.M.B.
2. File.                 9. 63rd. Fld. Coy, R.E.
3. War Diary.           10. 107th. Coy, R.A.S.C.
4.    "                 11. Bde. Signalling Officer.
5. 1/4th. R.S.F.        12. Lowland Division "Q"
6. 1/8th. S.R.          13. Staff Captain.
7. 9th. S.R.            14.   "      "    (Camp Duties.)
                        15. Provost Officer.

Army Form C. 2118.

# WAR DIARY
or
## INTELLIGENCE SUMMARY.
*(Erase heading not required.)*

Instructions regarding War Diaries and Intelligence Summaries are contained in F.S. Regs., Part II. and the Staff Manual respectively. Title pages will be prepared in manuscript.

| Place | Date | Hour | Summary of Events and Information | Remarks and references to Appendices |
|---|---|---|---|---|
| BEDBURG. | AUGT. 1st. | | Training as usual. | |
| | 2nd. | | Party of 5 Officers and 100 O.Rs. (representatives of each Battn.) left here for NIDEGGEN to take part in IV Corps Torchlight Tattoo to be held on 16th. inst. | |
| | 3rd. | | Church Parades. | |
| | 4th. | | General Holiday. Brigadier General E.S. GIRDWOOD, C.B., C.M.G. returned from leave and resumed Command of the Brigade vice Lt. Colonel C. GIBB, 1/4th. R.S.F. A concert was given by "A Miss Lena Ashwell Concert Party" in the Y.M.C.A. Hall, BEDBURG. | |
| | 5th. | | Training as usual. Neurath and PRIMMERSDORF passed from Comdt. B. Sub-Area to Comdt.C.Sub-Area for purposes of Civil Administration. Riding Classes cancelled owing to Lt. G.E. Potter, M.C. 7th. Queen's Own Hussars proceeding to Division. A lecture was given at KONIGSHOVEN by Rev. G.H. HEASLET on "Venereal Diseases" | |
| | 6th. | | Training as usual. Lecture was given at NEURATH by the Rev. G.H. Heaslet on "Venereal Diseases" | |
| | 7th. | | Training as usual. | |
| | 8th. | | Detachment of 5 Officers and 220 O.Rs. of 1/8th. S.Rs. left KONIGSHOVEN for HERBESTHAL to take over Frontier Post from HIGHLAND Division. Brigade School closed. | |
| | 9th. | | Training as usual. | |
| | 10th. | | Church Parades. | |
| | 11th. | | Training as usual. (Tennis Tournament was held by this Brigade in BEDBURG) | |
| | 12th. | | Training as usual. | |
| | 13th. | | Training as usual. | |
| | 14th. | | Part of No.II Sub-Area was taken over by No.3 Sub-Area Comdt. at 10.00 hours to-day who will administer the whole as "B" Sub.Area. A Lecture was given by Rev. C.E.R. WHEELER at BEDBURG on "PALESTINE CAMPAIGN" | |
| | 15th. | | Training as usual. A Representative Party of all ranks from Units in this Area attended IV Corps Torchlight Tattoo as spectators. A play was given in Y.M.C.A. Hall, BEDBURG by a "Miss Lena Ashwell Dramatic Coy." | |
| | 16th. | | Training as usual. A Representative Party of all ranks from Units in this Area attended IV Corps Torchlight Tattoo as spectators. | |
| | 17th. | | Church Parades. A mounted paper chase was given by 1/8th. S.Rs. at KONIGSHOVEN. | |
| | 18th. | | Training as usual. Order received that 5 Officers and 100 O.Rs. of 1/4th. R.S.F. would relieve attachment of 1/8th. S.Rs. at HERBESTHAL on 21/8/19. Units concerned were notified. Lt(Temp.Capt.) E.R. SALTONSTALL, M.C. returned from leave and resumed duty of Staff Captain vice Capt. BACON, M.C. Party of 5 Officers and 100 O.Rs. performers at IV Corps Torchlight Tattoo NIDEGGEN returned | |

Army Form C. 2118.

# WAR DIARY
## or
## INTELLIGENCE SUMMARY.

*(Erase heading not required.)*

Instructions regarding War Diaries and Intelligence Summaries are contained in F. S. Regs., Part II. and the Staff Manual respectively. Title pages will be prepared in manuscript.

| Place | Date | Hour | Summary of Events and Information | Remarks and references to Appendices |
|---|---|---|---|---|
| BEDBURG. | Augt. 18th. | | (Contd.) to their Units to-day. | |
| | 19th. | | Training as usual. | |
| | 20th. | | Training as usual. Warning Order received that 1/8th. & 9th. S.Rs. would probably proceed to the CURRAGH, IRELAND about 27/8/19. Units concerned were warned accordingly. 9th.S.R. & 63rd. Fld. Coy. Sports held at NEURATH. | |
| | 21st. | | Training as usual. Relief of 1/8th. S.Rs. at HERBESTHAL by 1/4th. R.S.F. was completed to-day. Mounted Paper Chase was held by Bde. Hqrs. | |
| | 22nd. | | Training as usual. Wire received from Division that 1/8th. & 9th. S.Rs. would entrain on 1st. & 2nd. Sept. respectively. Units concerned were informed accordingly. "FANCIES" Concert Party gave an Entertainment in Y.M.C.A. Hall, BEDBURG. | |
| | 23rd. | " | Training as usual. "PEDLERS" Concert Party gave an Entertainment in Y.M.C.A. Hall, BEDBURG. | |
| | 24th. | | Church Parade. | |
| | 25th. | | Training as usual. Battery | |
| | 26th. | | Training as usual. D/ 51.R.F.A. held a Mounted Paper Chase/ at KONIGSHOVEN. | |
| | 27th. | | Training as usual. | |
| | 28th. | | Training as usual. Information received that Division would probably entrain between 23rd. and 28th. September, 1919. | |
| | 29th. | | Training as usual. 3rd. Lowland Brigade Headquarter held a Mounted Paper Chase. All Units were invited. | |
| | 30th. | | Training as usual. Major A.P. Bowen, M.C. Brigade Major, proceeded on 28 days leave to U.K. | |
| | 31st. | | Church Parades. B.G.C.'s farewell speech to 1/8th. & 9th. Scottish Rifles. | |

1/9/19.
\*\*\*\*\*\*

[signature]
Brigadier General,
Commanding 3rd. Lowland Inf. Brigade.
\*\*\*\*\*\*\*\*\*\*\*\*\*\*\*\*\*\*\*\*\*\*\*\*\*\*\*\*\*\*\*\*\*\*

# 3RD. LOWLAND INFANTRY BRIGADE

Transfer of 1/8th. & 9th. Scottish Rifles
to the United Kingdom.

## GENERAL INSTRUCTIONS NO.1.

### STORES.

1. The equipment and stores of the 1/8th. & 9th. S.Rs. as enumerated in Lowland Division Instructions will entrain on Augt. 31st. as per attached table "A".

### PERSONNEL.

2. Personnel of 1/8th. & 9th. S.Rs will entrain as per Table "B" attached.

### ENTRAINING.

3. Each Battalion will detail 1 Officer to report to R.T.O. as Assistant at both entraining and detraining station.
Entraining state will be prepared showing:-
    (1) Number of Officers and Other Ranks.
    (2) Number of vehicles 4 wheeled limbered.
    (3) Number of vehicles 4 wheeled not limbered.
    (4) Number of vehicles 2 wheeled.
    (5) Amount of baggage in tons, stores, etc, other than in vehicles.
Copies of this state will be handed to the R.T.O. and the Staff Entraining Officer. All vehicles, packages, etc, are to be clearly marked with name of unit. All packages must be securely packed.

### LOADING PARTIES.

4. Each Battalion will detail 2 Officers and 75 Other Ranks to load up their vehicles and stores. These parties will report to the R.T.O. HARFF. Station 3½ hours before time of departure of train, and will work entirely under his orders.

### ADVANCE PARTIES.

5. Advance Parties of 1 Officer and 30 O.Rs., from each Battalion will report to R.T.O. Harff at 10.00 hours on day of departure.

### GUARDS.

6. A Guard of 1 Officer, 1 C.Q.M.S. and 6 O.Rs, will be detailed to accompany each Battalion's Baggage and Equipment to ENGLAND.
Unless the equipment is proceeding by barge, in which case this guard will be despatched to rejoin their battalion in the U.K. by steamship on their arrival at ANTWERP.
A list of packages despatched by each Unit will be forwarded in quadruplicate to Bde. H.Q.

### REQUISITIONED STORES.

7. These will be handed in to the local Burgomaster and a detailed receipt obtained in triplicate. Particular attention is drawn to Low. Div. Instruction Addendum No.3 as to the method of returning requisitioned articles and the pro forma to be used.

### RATIONS.

8. Battalions will entrain with the unconsumed portion of day's ration and two complete day's rations (including 1 Train Ration) Every Officer and man will also carry his Iron Rations.

2.

### Rations (Contd.)

The train ration will be delivered by R.A.S.C. at Harff Station to Battalions on morning of departure. Hot water will be obtainable at all HALTE REPAS viz, HUY, CHARLEROI, GHISLENGHIEN and HERRIS.

Battalions will arrange to send cooking utensils with equipment guard proceeding to Antwerp as the HALTE REPAS on this line are closed.

### BAGGAGE.

9. Two lorries to convey baggage to personnel trains will report at each Battalion Headquarters at 08.00 hours on day of departure.

### TRAIN PICQUETS.

10. Battalions will each detail a train picquet for front and rear of train, these picquets will be posted at all HALTE REPAS and will not allow any soldiers to leave the station precincts, or to enter any other train which may be near.

### ACCOUNTS.

11. All outstanding accounts, Canteen, etc., are to settled by Units before departure.

ACKNOWLEDGE.

*E.R. Blackerstall.*
Captain,
Staff Captain,
3rd. Lowland Infy. Bde.

29-8-19.

Copies to:-

| | |
|---|---|
| B.G.C. | 1. |
| B.M. | 1. |
| S.C. | 2. |
| S.C.C.D. | 1. |
| 1/8th. S.R. | 3. |
| 9th. S.R. | 3. |
| 107th. Coy, R.A.S.C. | 2. |
| D.A.P.M. | 2. |
| Low. Div. Train. | 1. |
| Low. Div. "Q" | 1. |
| Low. Div. "G" | 1. |
| D.A.D.V.S. | 1. |
| A.D.M.S. | 1. |
| C.R.A. | 1. |
| C.R.E. | 1. |
| Canteen Officer. | 1. |
| WAR DIARY | 2 |

3rd. Lowland Infantry Brigade.

Table "A" issued with General Instructions No.1.

## Equipment trains.

| Train No. | Serial No. | Unit. | Strength. Axles. | Entrain Station. | Composition. Flats. Covers. Coach. | | | Depart. | Date. | Destination. |
|---|---|---|---|---|---|---|---|---|---|---|
| S. | H.B.201. | 1/8th.S.R. | 38. | Harff. | 10. | 4. | 1. | 15.51. | 31/8/19. | Antwerp. |
| S. | H.B.202. | 19th.S.R. | 38. | Harff. | 20. | 8. | 1. | 13.51. | 31/8/19. | Antwerp. |

All Vehicles and baggage must be at entraining station 3 hours before advertised time of departure.
All vehicles and baggage must be clearly marked with the serial number allotted to Unit.

3rd. Lowland Infantry Brigade.

Table "B" issued with General Instructions No.1.

## Personnel Trains.

| Train No. | Serial No. | Unit. | Strength. Off. | Strength. O.R. | Entraining Station. | Depart. | Date. | Destination. |
|---|---|---|---|---|---|---|---|---|
| 9. | A.O.254. | 1/8th.S.R. | 25. | 560. | HAREE. | 12.12. | 1/9/19. | CALAIS. |
| 10. | A.O.255. | 9th.S.R. | 25. | 575. | HAREE. | 12.12. | 2/9/19. | CALAIS. |

Notes.

(1) Units must be at Entraining Station 1 hour before advertised time of departure.
(2) No soldier will detrain until ordered by an Officer.
(3) All doors of trucks on right hand side (left hand side in Germany) will be kept closed.
(4) Brake vans must not be used for personnel or baggage.
(5) Carriages and station premises will be kept clean.
(6) The R.T.O. is in supreme control of the station, his decision on all matters relating to railway working or station precincts is final.

Duplicate

MG 30/4 Low Bde

Army Form C. 2118.

# WAR DIARY
## or
## INTELLIGENCE SUMMARY.

(Erase heading not required.)

Instructions regarding War Diaries and Intelligence Summaries are contained in F. S. Regs., Part II. and the Staff Manual respectively. Title pages will be prepared in manuscript.

| Place | Date | Hour | Summary of Events and Information | Remarks and references to Appendices |
|---|---|---|---|---|
| BEDBURG, GERMANY. | Sept. 1st. | | Training as usual. | |
| | 2nd. | | Training as usual. | |
| | 3rd. | | Training as usual. Letter received from Division saying that Bde.H.Q. would probably be broken up and 1/4th.R.S.F. & T.M.B. administered direct from Division H.Q. Units concerned were notified accordingly. | |
| | 4th. | | Training as usual. Captain P.R. MARGETSON, M.C., 1/4th. Royal Scots Fusiliers assumed temporary command duties as Brigade Major vice Major A.P. BOWEN, M.C. who proceeded on leave on 31/8/19, and Temporary Staff Captain, vice Captain E.R. SALTONSTALL, M.C. who proceeded to 1st.Bde. to-day. | |
| | 5th. | | Training as usual. Representatives from all units and one from Bde. H.Q. attended Conference of War Office officials at DUREN on "Demobilization Forms." A Mounted Paper chase was held by this Bde. H.Q. | |
| | 6th. | | Lt.Col. JEFFCOTT, Lowland Division visited G.O.C. in order to make necessary arrangements to Break up Bde.H.Q. Training as usual. | |
| | 7th. | | Church Parades. | |
| | 8th. | | Training as usual. Orders received that Bde.H.Q. would be disbanded at 12.00 hours on 9th.inst and that 1/4th. R.S.F. and T.M.B. would become Divisional Troops. | |
| | 9th. | | Bde.H.Q. disbanded at 12.00 hours. | |

P. Kingston Capt
For BRIGADIER GENERAL
COMMANDING
3RD. LOWLAND INFANTRY BRIGADE.

Army Form C. 2118.

# WAR DIARY
## or
## INTELLIGENCE SUMMARY.
*(Erase heading not required.)*

Instructions regarding War Diaries and Intelligence Summaries are contained in F. S. Regs., Part II. and the Staff Manual respectively. Title pages will be prepared in manuscript.

| Place | Date | Hour | Summary of Events and Information | Remarks and references to Appendices |
|---|---|---|---|---|
| BEDBURG, GERMANY. | Sept. 1st. | | Training as usual. | |
| | 2nd. | | Training as usual. | |
| | 3rd. | | Training as usual. Letter received from Division saying that Bde.H.Q. would probably be broken up and 1/4th.R.S.F. & T.M.B. administered direct from Division H.Q. Units concerned were notified accordingly. | |
| | 4th. | | Training as usual. Captain P.R. MARGETSON, M.C., 1/4th. Royal Scots Fusiliers assumed temporary command duties as Brigade Major vice Major A.P. BOWEN, M.C. who proceeded on leave on 31/8/19, and Temporary Staff Captain, vice Captain E.R. SALTONSTALL, M.C. who proceeded to 1st.Bde. to-day. | |
| | 5th. | | Training as usual. Representatives from all units and one from Bde. H.Q. attended Conference of War Office Officials at DUREN on "Demobilization Forms." A Mounted Paper Chase was held by this Bde. H.Q. | |
| | 6th. | | Lt.Col. JEFFCOTT, Lowland Division visited G.O.C. in order to make necessary arrangements to break up Bde.H.Q. Training as usual. | |
| | 7th. | | Church Parades. | |
| | 8th. | | Training as usual. Orders received that Bde.H.Q. would be disbanded at 12.00 hours on 9th.inst and that 1/4th. R.S.F. and T.M.B. would become Divisional Troops. | |
| | 9th. | | Bde.H.Q. disbanded at 12.00 hours. | |

*[signature]*
BRIGADIER GENERAL
COMMANDING
3RD. LOWLAND INFANTRY

www.ingramcontent.com/pod-product-compliance
Lightning Source LLC
Chambersburg PA
CBHW081451160426
43193CB00013B/2447